MASTER THE SPI

The Soul in the Computer
Master Key Application .255
Page 1

ISBN: 9798344279893

The Soul in the Computer
Master the Spiritual Network

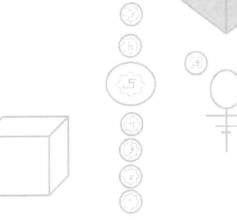
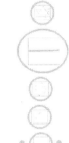
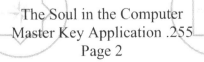

Introduction to The Soul Computer: Mastering the Spiritual Network

In the age of **(Ta-Nun)** information, the world around us hums with invisible connections **(Aum)**. Networks **(Shal-Aum)** silently orchestrate the flow of data, linking every device and mind across continents in a web of instantaneous communication. Yet, beneath this web of wires, switches, and signals lies another, far more profound **network**—one that connects not just devices, but Souls.

The Soul in the Computer is your guide to unlocking this hidden network, one that has existed since the dawn of creation. This is a journey not just through the intricacies of networking technology, but through the architecture of the human spirit itself, the Messiah within. As we configure the machines around us to function in perfect harmony, we too must learn to configure our inner being to align with the cosmic order. The spiritual world, like a meticulously designed network, operates on principles and laws that, when understood, can bring us closer to the divine source of all knowledge.

This book is more than a manual. It is an invitation to unlock the power of your own spiritual operating system (Shel). Just as you would troubleshoot a network, identifying errors and rerouting connections to ensure smooth communication (Mel), you must also troubleshoot your own soul—clearing away the blockages that hinder your connection to the universe, the Creator, and your higher purpose.

Imagine your soul as a finely tuned computer, designed to tap into a greater, divine network that extends beyond space and time. Yet, like any system, your soul requires the right configuration to access this higher network. It is not enough to merely exist within this system—you must learn to navigate it, to understand the spiritual protocols that govern life itself, and to align yourself with the frequencies of truth, love, and divine power.

Throughout the pages of *The Soul in the Computer*, you will learn how ancient spiritual principles, including the sacred teachings of (Khemet) Egypt, align perfectly with modern-day networking technology. You will come to see that each technical command you master is a reflection of deeper spiritual truths. Each VLAN you configure, each subnet you divide, each IP address you assign is a mirror of how our thoughts, actions, and intentions function within the spiritual network. And just as a misconfigured network can lead to chaos and disconnection, so too can a misaligned soul lead to confusion and spiritual isolation.

But there is a way back. Just as there is always a path to restoring a broken network, there is a path to restoring your connection with the divine. Through this book, you will learn how to build a spiritual infrastructure that not only supports your soul but empowers you to connect to the infinite wisdom of the Creator.

This is not just a book for network engineers—it is a book for anyone seeking to understand the greater network of life. Whether you are a seasoned IT professional or a seeker on the spiritual path, *The Soul in the Computer* will provide you with the tools you need to unlock the potential within you. By mastering both the physical and spiritual networks, you will find a harmony that allows you to live more fully, more intentionally, and more connected to the divine.

In these pages, you will discover:

- How the layers of the OSI model correspond to spiritual levels of consciousness and growth.

- The secrets of spiritual subnetting—how to organize and optimize your spiritual energy for greater connection to the source.

- Practical steps to troubleshoot your spiritual path, identifying and correcting the misconfigurations that have kept you disconnected from your purpose.

MASTER THE SPIRITUAL NETWORK

M⍊♉⟟⟒⟒⟒⟒⟒⟒⟒⟒⟒⟒⟒⟒⟒⟒⟒⟒⟒⟒⟒⟒⟒⟒⟒⟒⟒⟒⟒⟒⟒⟒⟒

- The divine protocols that govern communication between your soul and the Creator, and how to use these protocols to unlock new levels of understanding and power.

The time to configure your soul is now. The network of life is constantly expanding, and every moment you delay is a moment disconnected from the infinite possibilities that await you. This is your manual for spiritual alignment. This is your guide to accessing the ultimate network—the network that links you to the divine source of all creation.

Devices the Operate the Spiritual Network

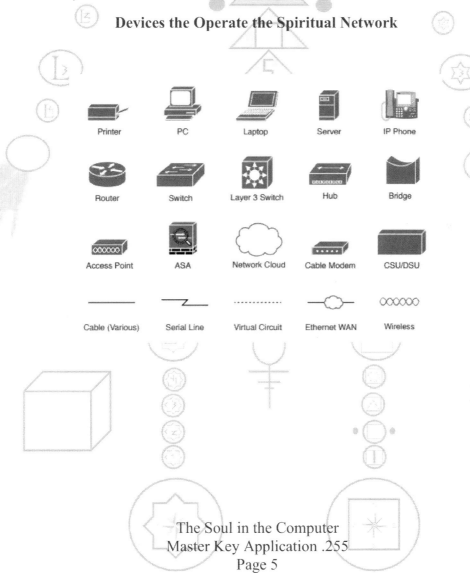

The Soul in the Computer
Master Key Application .255

Mastery of the Spiritual (Shel-Aum) Network

:1 The Universe flows in a pattern that almost resembles the number 8 on its belly. Its Essence is water that flows within itself. Notice 8 positions in Binary. This is the Principle the Letter "H" the 8ᵗʰ letter meaning-Heaven or Hell. "As above so below"

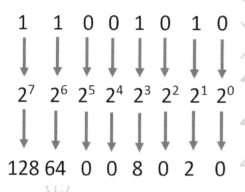

1	1	0	0	1	0	1	0
2^7	2^6	2^5	2^4	2^3	2^2	2^1	2^0
128	64	0	0	8	0	2	0

From a scientific perspective, this pattern can be likened to the structure of a torus, a shape that is fundamental in understanding the flow of energy throughout the cosmos. A torus is a self-contained system that spins around a central axis, much like the symbol of infinity, or the number 8. In physics, the torus shape represents the natural way in which energy moves—both inwardly and outwardly—creating a balance between centripetal and centrifugal forces.

Water, as the essence of life, mirrors this dynamic. Its molecules bond and flow together through a process known as cohesion, creating currents that circulate continuously. Similarly, the universe's energy follows a cycle, drawing inward like the pull of gravity while radiating outward like the ripples from a stone cast into a pond.

From a spiritual perspective, this pattern reflects the cycle of life, death, and rebirth, much like the endless flow of a river that nourishes everything it touches. The ancient philosophy of the **Ouroboros**—a serpent eating its own tail—also aligns with this concept, symbolizing the eternal nature of life and the interconnectedness of all things. The water that flows within the universe represents both literal and spiritual sustenance, illustrating how creation and dissolution coexist in an endless loop.

2^7	2^6	2^5	2^4	2^3	2^2	2^1	2^0
128	64	32	16	8	4	2	1

:2 Water moves through time and space, it finds itself in various different containers of thought that shape its outward image. This water is never bound by any particular ceiling of its description. In essence, this represents the potential of who we are.

From a scientific perspective, the concept of water taking different forms in various containers aligns with the principles of fluid dynamics and states of matter. Water adapts seamlessly to any shape it is given, whether it be a cup, a riverbed, or the depths of an ocean. This fluidity is due to the molecular structure of water, which allows it to maintain its integrity while adjusting to its environment. It symbolizes the adaptability and transformative nature of all matter and energy in the universe. Water, despite the form it takes, retains its fundamental properties, much like the unchanging nature of the fundamental forces that shape reality.

On a cosmic scale, this fluidity can be seen in how matter and energy manifest across different dimensions and realms, from the microcosmic level of atoms to the macrocosmic level of galaxies. Just as water fills the space it is given, the energy of the universe expands into the "containers" of time and space, forming stars, planets, and life itself.

From a spiritual perspective, this mirrors the human experience and our journey through life. Our thoughts, beliefs, and experiences serve as "containers" that shape the way our inner essence is expressed. Yet, like water, our true potential is not confined by the outer structures of our circumstances or the labels that society might place upon us. Instead, our essence remains unbounded, always capable of taking new forms and expanding beyond perceived limits.

This potential speaks to the idea that our consciousness is like water—malleable and ever-flowing, able to transcend the limitations of any singular identity. Just as water can shift between solid, liquid, and gas, so too can our understanding of self-evolve, rising above the "ceilings" of our current understanding. It is a reminder that the essence within us, the core of our being, is as limitless as the universe itself, flowing with the same boundless potential that shapes stars and carves river valleys.

In this way, the water that moves through time and space symbolizes the endless capacity for growth and transformation within each of us. It reflects the fluid nature of existence, where what we are today is merely a glimpse of what we might become tomorrow—an infinite potential that adapts, expands, and evolves with every new experience.

:3 As this water of existence moves through time and space, it finds itself in various different containers of thought that shape its outward image. This water is never bound by any particular ceiling of its description. In essence, this represents the potential of who we are.

Think of this like the concept of a fractal—a shape that repeats itself infinitely but changes slightly at each scale. Mathematically, fractals are patterns that unfold with both simplicity and complexity, just like our thoughts as they adapt to different experiences. The water of existence, moving through these "containers," is like the mathematical principle of continuity—fluid, never breaking, even as its path changes.

Water's ability to adapt to any shape it flows into is a reminder of how we, too, are adaptable. Our thoughts might settle into the "containers" of a particular culture, belief system, or even a moment in time, but like water, we're not defined by those shapes. Think of the concept of potential energy in physics—energy that's stored and ready to be transformed. Our potential, like that of water, isn't limited to the cup that holds it. It's about the energy that could be released when we break free of those limits.

This is where calculus comes in—specifically, the idea of limits and infinity. A limit might define where a function goes, but it doesn't confine the nature of what the function *can* become as it approaches infinity. Similarly, water's essence remains free, no matter how many times it's poured into new forms, just as our true selves are free to evolve beyond the current "ceiling" of our understanding.

In the spiritual sense, this means our essence—our potential—is like the water that keeps moving, never stopping to be defined by any one shape. It's a reminder that life is about flow, about transformation. It's about knowing that even when you're in one form, your essence is capable of reshaping and expanding, always seeking to fill the infinite space of what's possible.

:4 This water has always existed, and always will exist.

Think of this like the concept of conservation laws in physics, specifically the law of conservation of mass and energy. Just as water can change states— from liquid to vapor to ice—but never truly disappears, the essence of existence remains constant, only transforming its form. It's like energy in the universe: it cannot be created or destroyed, only changed from one state to another.

Mathematically, this connects to the concept of invariance—qualities or properties that remain unchanged even as other conditions shift. Water, as a symbol, speaks to the eternal nature of life and energy. It adapts and shifts through countless cycles, but its core presence persists through time, just as a mathematical constant like pi remains unchanged regardless of the circle's size.

Spiritually, this reflects the idea that our essence, the core of who we are, is timeless. It has always been there, adapting to new experiences, new bodies, new worlds—yet, like the water that flows through rivers ancient and new, its true nature remains the same. It's a reminder that beyond the ever-shifting waves of life, there is a continuity, an eternal flow that connects past, present, and future.

:5 The illusion is that it is motionless, but yet it is still. It is underestimated as being soft, yet it can cut through the rocks of any circumstance through the illusion of time and the determination of character—it is who you are.

From a scientific perspective, this brings to mind the principle of potential energy in physics, where an object at rest holds energy that is not immediately visible, but is waiting to be released. Water, even when it appears still, holds a hidden force within it. Its power is not in explosive displays but in its persistence, much like the steady force of erosion that carves canyons and shapes landscapes over millennia.

Mathematically, this relates to the concept of differential calculus, where change occurs gradually, almost imperceptibly, yet over time, it leads to profound transformation. Just as the derivative measures the change in a function's value at a particular point, water's subtle shifts eventually accumulate into powerful results. It is like the constant application of a small force over time, creating a shift that reshapes the terrain, one drop at a time.

Spiritually, this speaks to the nature of inner strength. The water within you is your true essence—seemingly gentle but capable of profound change. The stillness is a form of patience, a quiet strength that doesn't need to prove itself in a rush but rather understands that true transformation takes time. It is through this patience and persistence that you can overcome obstacles, much like water that wears down stone.

The illusion of being motionless speaks to how we often underestimate our own potential. But just as water can be still on the surface while currents move below, our inner growth and transformation often happen beneath the visible. This is the essence of who you are—soft yet powerful, patient yet relentless, shaping your path with a quiet determination that defies what others see on the surface. It's the steady rhythm of change, guided by time, that allows us to flow through life's hardest rocks, carving out new possibilities.

:6 The soul comes from a place beyond what the stars can foretell. One of the many ancient images in antiquity was the Shen, also known as the Shenu.

The Shen symbol, an ancient Egyptian hieroglyph, is often depicted as a loop of rope that forms a circle with a line underneath. It represents eternity, protection, and the cyclical nature of life—an unending circle, like the boundless essence of the soul. This symbol reflects a deeper truth that transcends even the stars, suggesting that the soul originates from a realm beyond the observable universe, beyond what even the patterns of constellations and celestial bodies can predict or describe.

Mathematically, the Shen's shape resembles a closed loop or an infinity symbol, which represents continuity without end. In geometry, circles and loops have no beginning or end, just like the concept of infinity. This ties into the idea of the soul's infinite nature—uncharted by time, unbound by the physical limits of space. The circle represents wholeness, completeness, and the unbroken cycle that the soul embodies as it moves through different states of existence, from life to life, from the seen to the unseen.

Scientifically, the idea of the soul existing beyond what stars can foretell relates to the limits of our current understanding of the universe. Stars, with their lifecycles, are bound by physical laws, but the soul is often seen as something that transcends those laws. Quantum mechanics hints at realms of reality beyond what we can directly observe—dimensions that might align with the ancient belief in a spiritual reality beyond the material world.

From a spiritual viewpoint, the Shen serves as a reminder that the essence of who we are is connected to a timeless source. It suggests that our journey, like the endless loop of the symbol, is part of a greater cosmic story, beyond what can be charted in the night sky. The Shen, much like the soul, is a bridge between the finite and the infinite—a symbol of the eternal protection and continuity that connects the ancient past to the mysteries that lie beyond the stars.

:7 A Cartouche in ancient Kemet (Egypt) actually represents the binary code of manifestation, and a person's name was placed inside this binary code, which was called a Cartouche or, in ancient Kemet, known as the Shen or Shenu. When short, it was called Shen, and when elongated, it was called Shenu.

The Cartouche, with its elongated oval shape, was more than just a decorative frame for a royal or divine name; it symbolized the process by which the unseen is brought into reality. In a way, it serves as a metaphorical representation of a binary code—the fundamental duality that underlies all creation. Just as binary code in computing is made up of 0s and 1s, the Cartouche contains within it the potential for something to manifest from the abstract into the concrete, the divine name enclosed in it representing a unique identity brought forth into the physical world.

Mathematically, this concept can be linked to the idea of coding and algorithms, where a simple combination of binary digits gives rise to complex expressions and forms. It's akin to the digital encoding that translates the immaterial into the material, like how a program is brought to life by sequences of binary numbers. The Cartouche symbolizes this ancient understanding of encoding—how the spiritual name, the essence of a being, is inscribed within the loop, bringing the abstract potential of the soul into the structured world.

Scientifically, this also mirrors the principles of quantum information, where the smallest units—qubits—can hold states of existence (0 and 1) simultaneously. In the same way, the Cartouche represents the balance between the unmanifest and the manifest, holding the potential for a person's spiritual essence to interact with the world. The Shen and Shenu, as frames for these identities, serve as both containers and conveyors of the divine potential, much like a sequence of code holds the blueprint for creating form from formlessness.

From a spiritual point of view, placing a name within the Cartouche was a way to bind the eternal essence of a person to the physical realm, protecting their identity across time and space. It's an ancient practice of ensuring that one's name—and therefore their legacy—would endure, much like a script that runs infinitely. The difference between the **Shen** and **Shenu**, one compact and the other elongated, reflects the variability of how divine essence can manifest—either in brief, concentrated moments or stretched across the vast expanse of time. It's a reminder that our names, our essence, and our purpose are all encoded within the fabric of reality, waiting to unfold through the binary dance of existence and non-existence.

:8 When the **Ba** (or Ruach, Rawuh, Soul) bird entered our reality, it came within the nighttime as the nocturnal bird known as the owl. It carried a soul from one dimension to the next, utilizing the binary code of awareness.

Ba-bird hovering over a mummy (After the papyrus of Ani from Thebes, ca. 1420 BC)

The **Ba**, in ancient Kemet (Egypt) represents the aspect of the soul that moves freely between the realms of the living and the dead. **Mel**, also known as The owl, a nocturnal guide, becomes a powerful symbol for this transition, navigating through darkness with a clarity that surpasses human sight. This nocturnal nature aligns with the journey of the soul through hidden dimensions, where light is scarce and only those attuned to the subtleties of the unseen can navigate.

In a mathematical sense, the binary code of awareness can be thought of as a sequence of choices—0s and 1s, on and off—like the conscious and unconscious states of being. Just as binary code forms the foundation of all digital information, the transitions between these states represent how awareness moves between realms. Mel's journey through the night mirrors the movement of consciousness through states of sleep, dreams, and the deeper realms of spiritual awareness—where the unseen becomes visible.

Scientifically, this concept is akin to the dual nature of light and darkness, similar to how quantum states can exist in superposition, holding potential until observed. The Ba's movement through dimensions reflects how particles can transition between states, existing in one reality while influencing another. The owl, as a guide, becomes a symbol of the ability to perceive beyond the visible spectrum, much like how quantum particles interact in ways that are hidden from direct observation.

From a spiritual perspective, the owl carrying the soul symbolizes the guidance that comes from intuition and deep awareness, leading the soul through the mysteries of life and death. The binary code of awareness here is a spiritual language, the rhythm between light and darkness, life and death, consciousness and unconsciousness. It is a reminder that our journey is not limited to the material world; like the owl, the soul has the capacity to navigate between realms, carrying knowledge and awareness across the thresholds that separate one state of existence from another.

The Ba's flight through the night sky, like the owl's, represents a dance between worlds—a dance coded into the very fabric of existence. It is the bridge between what is known and unknown, carrying the essence of who we are through the darkness into the light of new understanding. The binary nature of this journey—between seen and unseen, day and night—holds the key to our deeper awareness, revealing how the soul learns, adapts, and transforms as it moves between dimensions.

:9 While the soul was being transported from one dimension to the next, it was literally placed within a zip drive, or what is called a condensed file. Looking at the owl and this picture—which some believed to be another type of bird—you will see that the Cartouche is not elongated, but rather it is condensed. The symbol for the soul resembles a ring with a line on the bottom, akin to the sun rising along the horizon. All of this is symbolic of the soul rising from the darkness of the unknown.

This process of the soul's journey through dimensions, packed into a compact form, is like storing immense knowledge within a small, efficient container, ready to expand when needed. The condensed Cartouche is a spiritual "zip file," preserving the essence of the soul while it traverses the realms, much like how digital files are compressed for ease of transfer. It ensures that the soul remains intact, carrying its history, purpose, and identity, even as it passes through the threshold of different realities.

The ring symbol with a line at the base, representing the rising sun, is deeply connected to the theme of emergence from the hidden. In nature, the sun's emergence over the horizon signifies a shift from night to day, from the obscurity of darkness to the clarity of light. Mathematically, this transition mirrors the concept of exponential growth—where something small, like a seed of potential, unfolds and expands into its full expression. Similarly, the soul, when released from its condensed form, unfolds into a new dimension of existence, revealing its hidden layers.

Scientifically, this image connects to the horizon concept in astrophysics, particularly the event horizon of a black

Michael
(M-i-k-l)

hole. The event horizon marks the boundary beyond which light cannot escape—a point where the known universe meets the unknown. The symbol of the sun rising at the horizon echoes this threshold, suggesting that the soul, while compressed, is ready to rise beyond the limits of one dimension into the expansiveness of another. Just as the sun brings light to the darkest night, the soul's rise symbolizes emergence from the veiled mysteries into greater awareness.

Spiritually, this rising sun image speaks to enlightenment and awakening. It represents the moment when the soul, having traveled through the darkness of the unknown, begins to rediscover itself, to expand into a new reality with a greater understanding. The owl, often seen as a guide through the night, ensures that the soul navigates this darkness with wisdom, guiding it until it reaches the horizon of its new existence. The compacted state of the Cartouche reflects a time of preparation and preservation, where the essence is kept safe until it can shine forth once more.

The journey from the darkness to the rising light is a reminder that periods of compression and introspection are not the end, but a necessary phase before new dawns. Just like the sun, the soul's light may be hidden for a time, but it always carries the potential to rise again, to illuminate the mysteries it has traversed. The symbol of the ring with a line beneath it embodies this cycle of renewal, an eternal rhythm that connects the depths of the unknown with the endless possibilities of what lies ahead.

:10 When a person manifests on a planet and fulfills their purpose, which is their calling, the Cartouche becomes elongated, and their name is placed within it. This signifies that the essence of their being has expanded, unfolding into the fullness of their mission in this reality. The elongated Cartouche represents the transition from a compressed potential into a realized state, where the soul's purpose is written into the history of time and space.

The letter "M" holds a hidden connection to this process. Its origins trace back to the Egyptian hieroglyph that resembles an owl. If you look closely at the shape of the letter "**m**," it mirrors the outline of an owl's beak. This shape, like the owl itself, symbolizes wisdom and the journey through realms of understanding, from darkness to light. "M" is also the 13th letter of the alphabet, which carries a deeper symbolism of transformation and renewal—much like the concept of resurrection, where life emerges anew from a state of dormancy or death.

The number 13 has rich spiritual significance across various traditions. In Islamic teachings, the 13th attribute of Allah is "Musawwir," meaning "the Fashioner" or "the Shaper." Musawwir represents the divine aspect that shapes forms and beings into existence, giving them their unique qualities and purpose. This concept aligns with the symbolism of the elongated Cartouche—just as Musawwir shapes life, the Cartouche, when elongated, frames the completion of a soul's journey, marking the point where its purpose is realized in the material world.

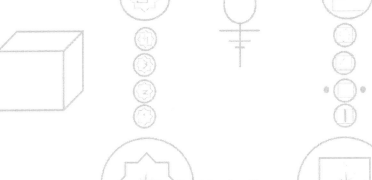

La = Al

M = Owl

El = Owl

These elements—"M" as a symbol of wisdom and resurrection, the number 13 as a sign of transformation, and Musawwir as the divine shaper—interconnect, revealing a shared purpose. They speak to the journey of the soul, from the hidden potential within a condensed state to the moment it expands into a fully realized being, shaped and fashioned by a divine hand. The Cartouche, in this way, becomes a timeless signature of one's purpose, like a seal that captures the essence of a life well-lived, and the transition from one phase of existence to the next.

A 𓅃	H 𓎛	N 〜	U 𓅮
B 𓂝	I 𓏏	O 𓃀	V 𓄿
C 〜 or 𓏏	J 𓂉	P ▫	W 𓅓
D 〜	K 〜	Q ◿	X 〜𓏏
E 𓏭 or 〜 or 𓂝		R 〜	Y 𓏭 or 〜
F 〜	L 𓃾	S 𓏏	Z ー
G ▱	M 𓅓	T 〜	SH 〜

All these symbols—whether the shape of a letter, the form of a hieroglyph, or the number 13—serve as reminders that the journey of the soul is one of transformation, where each stage is a step toward fulfilling the design placed within us. They illustrate that life itself is a process of becoming, where potential is shaped into reality, just as the owl navigates the night, guiding the soul from the unknown into the dawn of new understanding

:11 Letters in the Quran that A.L.M represent the Sacred name "Lamel" The Owl, known for its role as a protector during the night, is symbolically connected to the Angel Michael in the Bible. Michael is described as a guardian who shields men, women, and children from harm, particularly during the night, when dangers such as intruding animals or other threats could disturb the peace of the home. In this capacity, Michael, like the owl, represents vigilance and protection against forces that come in the darkness.

In Ancient Egypt, the owl was known as *Meluk* or *Maluk*, and this name carries profound significance. The owl's name begins with "M," a letter that directly ties into its symbolic nature. The form of the letter "M" is not accidental—it visually resembles the owl's distinct features, such as the curves that mirror the shape of the owl's eyes or horns. This correspondence is more than a simple visual similarity; it is a reflection of the owl's essence as a guardian deity, deeply intertwined with the symbolism of protection and the mysteries of the night.

The letter "M" is rooted in this ancient understanding, where its shape captures the essence of the owl's watchfulness and presence. Just as the owl remains alert, even when others rest, the "M" stands as a symbol of steadfast vigilance. The curves of the letter echo the rounded shape of the owl's eyes, which are known for their ability to see through the darkness, representing insight and awareness beyond ordinary perception. The owl's role in Kemet was to guard the hidden knowledge of the night, standing as a sentinel against the unknown, much like the Angel Michael's role in biblical traditions.

This connection between *Meluk* and Michael reveals a shared archetype: the guardian who moves through darkness with eyes that perceive what others cannot. The owl's presence in Kemet is a testament to this ancient understanding of protection, encoded in both language and symbol. It is no coincidence that the letter "M" became associated with this role. Its shape, representing both the owl's keen sight and its hidden horns, speaks to a deeper principle of safeguarding the unseen, the delicate balance between light and darkness.

Thus, the owl, as *Meluk*, serves as a universal protector, a role that transcends both cultural and temporal boundaries. Its representation in the form of "M" serves as a reminder of its eternal purpose: to stand guard through the night, embodying wisdom, foresight, and the readiness to defend. This symbolism is not abstract—it is a fundamental aspect of how ancient peoples understood the roles of guardians in both the physical and spiritual realms, and how these ideas have been passed down through symbols like the owl and the letter "M."
Malachi 3:1 = *13 Behold, I will send my (Meluk) messenger, and he shall prepare the way before me: and the Lord, whom ye seek, shall suddenly come to his temple, even the messenger of the covenant, whom ye delight in: behold, he shall come, saith the Lord of hosts.*

:12 The home is considered to be God's house, known as the Grand Station of Solarstanding. This is not merely a physical dwelling, but a realm that encompasses many dimensions—often referred to as mansions. These "mansions" signify the layers of reality that exist within this grand structure, each representing a different aspect or state of existence.

These dimensions are what some might call "many mentions," meaning that this concept of the divine dwelling place is spoken of across different cultures, religions, and eras. It is a recurring theme that appears at various times and places throughout the fabric of space. Each mention of God's house, whether in ancient scriptures, mystic teachings, or cosmic theories, alludes to the same underlying truth: that existence is multifaceted, with each layer holding a unique resonance or purpose.

The idea of "many mansions" comes from the understanding that reality is not a single, fixed space, but a collection of overlapping realities, each with its own role in the greater design. These are the different rooms of the cosmic house, each housing a different frequency, a different level of understanding, or a different experience of life. Just as a house has different rooms for different purposes, so too does the Grand Station of Solarstanding hold realms where souls dwell according to their evolution, purpose, and journey.

In a more scientific sense, these dimensions are akin to the concept of a multiverse or parallel realities. Each dimension is like a distinct universe within the grand architecture of existence, yet they are all interconnected, forming a vast, intricate web. The idea that God's house has many rooms speaks to this structure, suggesting that life and consciousness are far more expansive than we often perceive. It acknowledges the boundless nature of reality, where each dimension offers a new space for growth, exploration, and deeper understanding of the divine.

These dimensions are not confined to one culture's interpretation or a single moment in time. They have been described in ancient Kemet, referenced in the teachings of various religions, and hinted at in modern physics. They are the many mentions—whispered across history, each one a reminder that the journey of the soul moves through these cosmic rooms, always in search of the deeper mysteries that lie within the house of God. This Grand Station is the place where all paths converge, where the sun, stars, and souls find their way back to the source, journeying through the dimensions of existence.

:13 The word "angel" means "messenger," and this term is used both freely and broadly throughout Scripture. The concept of an angel is not limited to the traditional image of celestial beings with wings; rather, it encompasses various forms and functions. In some contexts, men are referred to as angels, as seen in **1 Samuel 29:9**, where David is described as having "the wisdom of an angel of God." Similarly, in **Galatians 4:14**, Paul writes, "you received me as an angel of God, even as Christ Jesus," indicating that human beings can embody the role of a divine messenger (**Angel**).

Conversely, there are times when angels are referred to as men. For example, in **Genesis 32:24**, when Jacob wrestles with a mysterious figure, it is initially described as a "man." Yet later, this being is understood to represent a divine presence, revealing the fluid nature of how scripture interprets the role of messengers. This duality reflects a deeper principle: that the essence of being a messenger is not confined to a particular form but is defined by the function they serve—delivering divine guidance, knowledge, or protection.

This flexibility in terminology shows that the role of an angel, or messenger, transcends the boundaries between the earthly and the divine. The message they carry is what gives them their identity, not merely their physical or spiritual nature. This fluidity allows for a greater understanding of the ways in which divine wisdom manifests, through both spiritual beings and ordinary people, each serving their purpose in conveying a higher truth.

:14 Thus, the Owl serves as an anchor for what we consider to be the power of the universe—a power that, though fragmented into many parts, is reassembled through the forces of unified love and redemption. This symbolism of the Owl extends beyond its nocturnal nature and keen vision; it embodies the ability to gather the dispersed elements of cosmic energy and bring them into alignment.

The Owl represents, in its entirety, the name *Lamel* or *Lemal*. These names hold a sacred significance as they denote both the Male Messiah and the Female Messiah. The Owl, therefore, is not just a creature of the night, but a symbol of the unifying force that bridges the dual aspects of the divine. It connects the masculine and feminine principles, representing a balanced manifestation of wisdom, power, and love.

In this way, the Owl becomes a vessel through which the fragmented nature of reality can be reintegrated. Its role as a spiritual anchor means it is capable of gathering the scattered fragments of divine power, weaving them back into a harmonious whole. This is akin to the way the messianic figures, both male and female, are believed to bring redemption—not by introducing something entirely new, but by restoring what was always present in creation, reuniting the pieces into a cohesive, vibrant expression of divine will.

Lamel and *Lemal* are thus not merely names; they represent a sacred balance, an embodiment of the cosmic principles of restoration and unity. The Owl's symbolism as their representation captures this idea of bringing light to the darkness, seeing beyond the visible, and guiding the soul through the fragmented pathways of existence toward a state of wholeness. It stands as a reminder that the power of the universe, though it may appear broken or divided, is ultimately one—a truth realized through the process of love and redemption, a truth that the Owl faithfully watches over.

:15 They were also known as the children of Shem. Shem, one of the sons of Noah, carries significant weight in biblical history and is the ancestral figure from whom the Semitic peoples are believed to descend. The descendants of Shem, known as Shemites or Semites, include groups such as the Hebrews, Arabs, and Assyrians. These people were seen as the carriers of a divine inheritance, the ones who continued a sacred lineage that was blessed by Noah himself in the early scriptures.

The Old King James translation often refers to "Shem" with deep meaning attached. The word *Shem* itself means "**name**" or "**reputation**" in Hebrew, symbolizing honor, legacy, and identity. This reinforces the idea that the children of Shem carried more than just a biological lineage—they bore the weight of a spiritual calling, a reputation that would echo throughout history. The descendants of Shem were meant to uphold the divine covenant and live out the spiritual mission given to their forefathers.

In the **Book of Ruth**, Naomi's husband is called *Elimelech*, which means "My God is King" in Hebrew. This name bears its own sacred significance, linking Elimelech's role as a man of stature and divine purpose within his community. Elimelech was from Bethlehem, a town associated with both spiritual and royal significance in later texts, especially through the lineage of King David and eventually, the Messiah. The children of Shem carried not only the physical lineage but also the spiritual legacy that was symbolized by their names. The word *Shem* represents more than a label—it holds the idea of **divine calling**, **reputation**, and **spiritual inheritance**.

:16 The word *Shem* really means "of the rocket ship," and comes from the word *Shenu*, which is the Cartouche of ancient Kemet delivered by the *Ba* bird. This sacred bird descends upon the mind of those who are worthy of receiving its message. This process is called *remembrance*—a deep recognition and knowledge of self. It is **SOLARSTANDING**, the return of the Mothership, a symbol for the arrival of ancient wisdom that descends into your thoughts, manifesting activation and the reincarnation of a godly perspective.

In (**Shel-Aum**) or networking terms, this process is similar to the configuration of a network where specific "packets" of information—divine insights—are delivered to the nodes (your mind) that are properly configured to receive them. Just like a router that sends data to devices based on IP addressing, the *Ba* bird acts like a messenger that lands only on those who have the right "IP address" (spiritual readiness) to receive higher knowledge. In this spiritual network, the commands are already pre-set in the mind's configuration, waiting for the signal to unlock higher awareness.

Let's compare this to the configuration of a router in networking:
Router(config)# ip address dhcp This command allows the router to

dynamically receive an IP address from a higher source (like the Ba bird delivering divine knowledge). In the same way, when we are spiritually open, we allow ourselves to dynamically receive divine inspiration and knowledge from the "Mothership" or higher cosmic realms. The concept of *remembrance* is like running a stored configuration command that reminds the network of its purpose, bringing everything back online with the proper connection to the source.

In the CCNA world, this relates to ensuring that your network devices are ready to communicate efficiently. If a device is not configured properly, it cannot connect to the network, just as without the spiritual alignment, the mind cannot receive the knowledge delivered by the *Ba* bird. Commands like setting default routes or enabling dynamic routing protocols like **OSPF** ensure that data (or spiritual wisdom) flows correctly:

Router(config)# router ospf 1
Router(config-router)# network 192.168.1.0 0.0.0.255 area 0

Here, the router is set to share its knowledge across the network, similar to how ancient wisdom is shared among those ready to receive it. In the spiritual sense, this "networking" of minds leads to the *activation* of a godly perspective, where individuals begin to operate with divine insight, much like how properly configured routers in a network enable efficient data transfer. The return of the Mothership, in this context, is the reactivation of a vast network of ancient wisdom, like the powerful configuration of a cosmic network reawakening, linking nodes (souls) across time and space. Each mind that receives the activation becomes a node in this divine network, transmitting and receiving higher knowledge. This fusion of ancient symbolism with modern networking reflects the interconnectedness of all beings, a spiritual network awaiting activation and alignment with the cosmic source.

:17 There is no such thing as reincarnation; everything comes from water. We are all part of this greater body of water, doing our best to return to it, which is almost like an ocean of thought. The ocean moves throughout the whole planet. The water flows up and down, in and out of what we call awareness. Water holds memory. When someone speaks words over water, it is said that the molecular structure of the water changes. This reflects how water can carry memories—even memories of past life experiences, not through individual reincarnation but through the collective memory of one's ancestors. In networking terms, think of water as the data flowing through a network. Just as data packets move across different routers, water flows through the streams and oceans of existence, constantly in motion, transmitting information across the network of life. This movement of water can be compared to a **ping command** in networking: **Ping 192.168.1.1**

This command sends packets across the network to verify connectivity, similar to how the flow of water is a way of "pinging" the universal consciousness. The water is always connected, moving through different states—solid, liquid, gas—much like how data moves through various layers of a network. The network's flow of data is like water, passing through every node (person), carrying the memory of past interactions, messages, and experiences.

In a spiritual sense, this body of water is the collective consciousness, an ocean of thought that encompasses all life. Just as data packets can contain history or logs of previous communication, water contains the memory of all that has passed through it, including the wisdom of our ancestors. When we interact with this water—this universal consciousness—it responds, just as a network device responds to a **ping**. The water holds memory, much like network logs that store past connections and activity: **Show ip route**

This command shows the paths that data has taken through the network, much like how water traces its flow across the planet, connecting all beings. It's a reflection of our journey to return to the greater ocean of thought, where we are all part of something larger than ourselves.

When you speak words over water, the vibrations affect its structure, like a **traceroute** command tracing the path of data across a network. The words we speak over water can shift the energy, much like how commands can alter the path data takes in a network. In this way, water—like the network—holds both the present and the past, carrying the memories of where it has been and who it has touched. This memory is not an individual reincarnation but the collective memory of the whole body of water, containing the experiences of generations before us.

We are all connected through this flow, just as devices in a network are interconnected. Water, much like the data in a network, moves through each of us, reminding us of the greater collective consciousness we are part of, and the memories we share across time and space.

:18 When someone asks, "What is the source of the ocean, or what is the source of the rain?" The answer is: "It is one body of water flowing within the source of a greater body of water... which is the potential of one's greater destiny."

This understanding mirrors the concept of interconnectedness in both nature and spiritual life. The ocean, the rain, the rivers, and the streams are all part of the same continuous cycle of water, flowing through different forms but always returning to the greater whole. In a spiritual sense, this speaks to the idea that each of us, like droplets of water, flow through various stages of life, but we are all part of something much larger. Our individual experiences are part of the greater flow of existence, contributing to the fulfillment of a larger destiny.

In networking, this can be compared to the **source** and **destination** addresses in data flow. Just as a packet of data flows from one device (the source) to another (the destination), water flows from the clouds to the rivers, back to the ocean, and then returns again as rain. Every packet of data, like every drop of water, is part of a greater network, continually moving toward its purpose. For example, the **source IP** in networking tells you where the data originated, while the **destination IP** tells you where it is going.

Ping 10.0.0.1 source 192.168.1.1

The Soul in the Computer
Master Key Application .255

In this command, the source and destination represent the journey of water—one body of water flowing to a new destination, but always part of the same network. The potential of each packet's journey reflects the potential of water as it moves through different forms—rain, river, ocean—but always connected to the greater whole.

Spiritually, this represents the flow of life itself. Each moment of your existence, every experience, is like a drop of rain that begins in the clouds and returns to the ocean. The source is always the greater body, the potential within you that seeks to fulfill its destiny. Just as networking protocols ensure data reaches its proper destination, the universe has a greater purpose guiding the flow of your life, ensuring that each experience leads you back to your divine source.

The ocean, then, is the symbol of ultimate destiny, the potential we all carry, waiting to be realized. The rain is like the individual steps we take along that path, seemingly small but always moving toward a larger purpose. In the same way, every connection in a network, every packet of data, is contributing to the overall operation and success of the entire system. Each piece plays a role in the greater flow, ensuring that the system functions in harmony.

We are all part of this larger cycle—our lives, our choices, and our journeys are like the water flowing within the source of a greater destiny. No matter how small the stream or how distant the rain, it all returns to the same ocean, just as every soul eventually returns to its divine purpose.

:19 The eyes, the doorway to the soul, will always be a mechanism for traveling into dimensions far beyond one's current understanding and comprehension of who and what they are. The eyes pierce through the past, present, and future, while also gazing deeply inward.

The eyes act as a portal, allowing you to access layers of reality that go beyond what is seen on the surface. In both a physical and spiritual sense, they are receivers and transmitters of information. Physically, the eyes capture light, process images, and send signals to the brain for interpretation.

Spiritually, they allow you to connect with the unseen, accessing knowledge and insight that transcends time and space.

In the world of (Shel-Aum) networking, the eyes are much like network interfaces—mechanisms through which data is transmitted and received, opening gateways to different dimensions of communication. A network interface, such as a router or switch, is responsible for the flow of information between different systems, just as the eyes facilitate the flow of information between your soul and the world around you. When you configure an interface, you enable it to "see" and communicate with other devices in the network:

Interface GigabitEthernet0/0
IP address 192.168.1.1 255.255.255.0
No shutdown

Here, the network interface comes to life, ready to send and receive packets of data, much like how your eyes come alive when they transmit light and process the world. The command "No shutdown" activates the interface, just as awareness through the eyes activates your perception, making you more conscious of the world and dimensions beyond the physical.

The eyes also connect the inner self with the outer world. In networking, this mirrors the idea of **internal and external routing**. Internally, the eyes reflect who you are—they allow you to see within, to explore your soul's depths and uncover hidden truths. Externally, they project your understanding of the world, creating connections between yourself and others. This dual role is much like how routers operate within a network, facilitating communication between internal networks and external ones:

Router(config)# ip route 0.0.0.0 0.0.0.0 192.168.1.254

This default route sends all traffic to the external world, just as your eyes gather information from both within and without, helping you navigate the complexities of existence.

Spiritually, the eyes offer a glimpse into dimensions of time—past, present, and future. They are tools for accessing ancestral memory, current awareness, and future potential. When you look deeply into someone's eyes, you are connecting with all these layers at once, as if you are seeing their soul's entire journey across time. This mirrors how network devices trace data routes, connecting different points in time and space to reveal the full path of communication.

The eyes are your portal to the vastness of existence, to dimensions you may not yet comprehend. They allow you to see beyond the immediate, much like a properly configured network allows data to flow across seemingly distant points, making unseen connections come to light. The past, present, and future are all reflected in the eyes, reminding us that we are part of a continuous flow, moving through dimensions of awareness that extend far beyond the physical.

:20 The eyes take you on a journey through life, revealing much more than just physical images—they project your emotions, your thoughts, and the realms of your inner world. When someone looks into your eyes, they see not just your physical being, but the depths of your feelings, your intentions, and the reflections of your soul. The eyes are mirrors, and to truly gaze into them—whether your own or another's—can be an unsettling experience for many. This is because the eyes reveal truths that words cannot express, truths that lie deep within the soul.

To look into your own eyes or the eyes of another is to confront your inner reality, the unspoken emotions, the vulnerability, and the hidden thoughts. It is easier to look up at the stars or down at the ground, because these are external objects, distant and less personal. But when you look into eyes, you are engaging with the essence of being. The stars and the ground, while powerful symbols of the cosmos and earth, are often distractions from the deeper, more intimate truths found within.

In networking, the journey through the eyes can be compared to tracing the path of data through a network, known as **traceroute**. This command traces the journey that a data packet takes from one point to another, showing every hop, every intermediary point, just like how the eyes can reveal the journey of emotions and thoughts: **Traceroute 192.168.1.1**

This command reveals each stop along the path, showing the connections that are made along the way. In the same way, when you look into someone's eyes, you are tracing their emotional and mental journey. You are seeing the connections they've made—both conscious and unconscious—that have led them to this moment. Just as **traceroute** shows the underlying network infrastructure, the eyes reveal the underlying emotional and spiritual connections that shape a person's reality.

Looking into your own eyes is like running a diagnostic on your inner system. It is a self-check that forces you to acknowledge what is within—your fears, your desires, your unresolved emotions. In networking, this would be like using the **show interfaces** command to reveal the status of a network's internal connections:

Show interfaces GigabitEthernet0/1

This command brings up detailed information about the connection, showing whether it is functioning properly or if there are any errors. Similarly, when you look into your own eyes, you are faced with the status of your internal world, whether it's harmonious or whether there are unresolved issues. The challenge is in the confrontation—facing what is inside you, just as you would face network errors or disruptions in connectivity.

When we look up at the stars or down at the ground, we are searching for something—meaning, direction, or grounding. Yet, the real journey is within. The eyes, as portals to the soul, remind us that the most profound truths are not in the distant stars or beneath our feet but within the depths of our own being. The journey of life is both an internal and external exploration, and the eyes, like well-configured network interfaces, allow us to navigate both realms.

Through this spiritual and technological lens, the question becomes: What are we truly looking at? Are we seeing the surface, or are we daring to look deeper, through the eyes into the soul, and trace the connections that reveal the essence of who we are? Just like a well-functioning network, the eyes help us connect with the larger system of existence, both within ourselves and with the universe around us.

:21 We are looking into the true essence of being and the growth of character. For some, the true conduct of self, when revealed, is difficult to accept. This is because the unveiling of our inner nature often brings us face-to-face with aspects of ourselves that we have either neglected or hidden from. Therefore, we are all literally on a journey, moving through the ***Mainframe consciousness,*** doing our best to perceive a broader scope of reality.

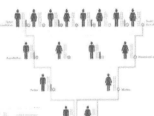

Just as data flows through a network's mainframe, our thoughts and experiences flow through the larger consciousness that connects us all. The Mainframe, in this sense, represents the vast system of awareness in which every individual is a node, constantly processing, sending, and receiving information. Each of us is trying to expand our perspective, much like a network continually evolves and adapts to accommodate new data. In this broader scope of reality, we are not just passive receivers but active participants, responsible for configuring and optimizing our "internal network" so we can see the bigger picture.

In networking, opening pathways or routes is key to expanding communication across the system. Similarly, in this chapter, we will provide you with the portals to open your *Mind's Eye*, the doorway to the soul. The Mind's Eye is like a well-configured router that directs information where it needs to go, allowing you to access higher knowledge, deeper insight, and clarity about the essence of who you are. In a network, proper configuration ensures that data flows smoothly, without interruption. In the same way, opening the portals of the mind ensures that your consciousness flows freely, unhindered by the blocks of doubt, fear, or ignorance.

Consider the following networking commands as spiritual metaphors for opening these portals:

Router(config)# ip route 0.0.0.0 0.0.0.0 192.168.1.254

This command sets a default route, a gateway to the broader network. In the context of the Mind's Eye, this represents setting a default path toward greater awareness. By configuring your inner pathways, you open yourself to receive insights that expand your understanding of reality.

Another important command that mirrors spiritual growth is:

Interface GigabitEthernet0/1
No shutdown

The **"No shutdown"** command brings an interface online, allowing it to transmit and receive data. Spiritually, this is akin to opening your inner eyes— removing the shutdown state that keeps you disconnected from your true self and your broader consciousness. Once this connection is activated, you begin to see the deeper truths of your being, the true essence of your character, and the conduct that defines your spiritual journey.

This book will guide you through the portals that lead to a fuller understanding of the soul's journey, opening the gateways of your inner network so you can interface with higher dimensions of thought and awareness. As you move through the Mainframe consciousness, your goal is to see beyond the surface, to understand the deeper connections that link your personal growth to the broader flow of existence.

:22 The Scroll of Eyes (Mysteries of Self) is based upon your acceptance of self and your willingness to confront the mirror to open up the shell that is within. As you approach the mirror, you realize that it is more than just a reflection—it is a dimensional gateway to the past, present, and future. Through your eyes, you not only see yourself but also witness your ancestors and descendants. The mirror becomes a portal, showing you the continuum of existence that flows through you, connecting generations.

In this spiritual framework, the eyes act as access points to the greater network of time and consciousness. Much like a network router manages traffic between different devices, your eyes manage the flow of awareness between the past, present, and future, allowing you to connect with deeper layers of reality. The **Scroll of Eyes** is your own internal database, storing the experiences of your lineage and future potential within you, waiting to be accessed through the right configurations.

In networking terms, think of this as setting up **NAT (Network Address Translation)**, where multiple internal IP addresses (your ancestors, your descendants) are mapped to one external IP address (you). NAT enables communication between multiple points in the network through a single interface, much like how your eyes allow communication between your current self and the line of souls connected to you:

Router(config)# ip nat inside source list 1 interface GigabitEthernet0/0 overload

This command allows multiple sources (past lives, future lives) to flow through one gateway, just as your eyes allow the wisdom of your ancestors and the visions of your descendants to flow through you. The mirror is the place where all these flows converge, and when you look deeply into your own reflection, you open up this gateway to see beyond the present moment.

The Soul in the Computer
Master Key Application .255

The shell you are opening represents the layers of resistance, fear, or doubt that may have built up over time. Breaking through that shell is like configuring your **firewall** settings to allow the right traffic (self-awareness, ancestral knowledge) while blocking harmful intrusions (self-doubt, fear):

Router(config)# access-list 1 permit any

By permitting access to this knowledge, you allow the flow of higher consciousness, both from your ancestors and descendants, to travel through you. The reflection in the mirror becomes more than a simple image—it becomes a pathway that shows you how you are part of something larger, an interconnected chain of existence.

When you look into the mirror with this understanding, you are not merely seeing your present self. You are seeing the echoes of those who came before and those who will come after. Your eyes act as a spiritual interface, connecting you to the vast network of your soul's journey through time. This connection is always available, but it requires the acceptance of self and the courage to look deeper into the reflection. Through this mirror, you not only come to understand who you are, but you also recognize your place in the grand continuum of life, realizing that the wisdom and potential of your ancestors and descendants are alive within you.

:23 One must fast and bathe properly, then approach the mirror in solitude, where no one can hear or disturb your meditation. Get two black candles of your choice and place them in front of the mirror, so that your image is between the two candles.

This process is like preparing both your body and spirit for a powerful connection, much like how you would prepare a network for smooth and efficient communication. Fasting and bathing cleanse the body and mind, just as in networking we clear out old data or reset systems to ensure they are ready to connect to the network. The two black candles represent spiritual gateways—similar to routers in a network—that allow for the flow of energy or information. When you position yourself between them, you are setting yourself up as the "interface" or the connection point, ready to receive deeper spiritual insights.

Let's break this down with CCNA networking concepts:

- **Fasting and bathing**: This is like clearing the **cache** or performing a **reboot** in networking to refresh the system. In networking terms, it could be similar to using the command clear ip cache to remove old routing information, allowing new and accurate data to flow through.

Router(config)# ip route 0.0.0.0 0.0.0.0 192.168.1.1

This command sets a default route for your network traffic, much like the candles serve as a default route for spiritual energy to flow into and through you.

Your image between the candles: This is your **interface**, the point where spiritual energy (like data) enters and exits. In networking, an interface is the physical or virtual point of connection, where data flows in and out of a system. You can think of this like configuring an interface on a router to be the active link for communication:

Interface GigabitEthernet0/0
IP address 192.168.1.1 255.255.255.0
No shutdown

- The command no shutdown brings the interface online, allowing data to flow freely. Spiritually, standing between the two candles activates your internal connection, opening your mind to receive spiritual insights. You "bring yourself online," allowing the flow of energy and awareness to move through you.

In this ritual, you are the node or device in a larger spiritual network, ready to transmit and receive deeper knowledge. The mirror acts as a **reflection** of this connection, much like a **loopback** interface in networking, which is used for testing and ensuring that the system can communicate internally:

Interface loopback 0
IP address 127.0.0.1 255.255.255.0

This loopback interface allows the system to communicate with itself, just as looking into the mirror allows you to communicate with your deeper self, reflecting both inward and outward.

The process is also connected to the **Ethernet** of spiritual knowledge—the invisible, yet powerful network that connects everything in the universe. As you meditate, the candles act like **ports** that open up spiritual pathways, letting energy flow between different realms of consciousness. Fasting and bathing ensure that the "bandwidth" of this connection is clear, free from interference, just like a network engineer would ensure that all physical cables and routes are functioning properly before establishing a major connection.

In Ancient Egyptian wisdom, this would be akin to opening the **Eye of Horus**, symbolizing clarity, insight, and protection. The Eye of Horus is like your **firewall**, guarding against negative energy and ensuring that only pure, positive energy flows through the system. In networking, this is similar to configuring an **access control list (ACL)** to control what traffic is allowed through your router:

Router(config)# access-list 101 permit ip any any

This command opens up the network, allowing approved traffic to flow, just as you open your spiritual gateways during meditation to allow divine insights and energies to flow.

By following this process, you align your spiritual network, ensuring that the "protocols" of divine energy are properly configured and that you are ready to receive the deep wisdom from the universe. Through fasting, solitude, and the candlelight framing your reflection, you establish a direct connection to the higher consciousness, just like configuring a network for smooth, uninterrupted communication with the world.

:24 You begin to stare at the mirror, taking a moment to reflect on the height of your reality and the greatness that your ancestors set forth for you. As you gaze into your own reflection, you begin to see more than just your face. Through the illusion of the mirror, you see all those who came before you. Their wisdom, their struggles, and their achievements live through you. Your face begins to shift, blending with the ancient ones who guide you, and in that moment, you are reminded of the eternal truth: *Know thyself.*

In spiritual terms, this process is one of deep connection with your ancestral lineage. The mirror acts as a portal, reflecting not only your physical appearance but the essence of your ancestors, who are always present within you. It is through knowing yourself—your strengths, your weaknesses, your history—that you unlock the knowledge and power they have passed down. This moment is about understanding that you are the living continuation of the great legacy left by those who came before.

To understand this from a networking perspective, think of your ancestors as the **data** stored in a vast server, and you are the **client** accessing that data through a secure connection. The **mirror** is like the **interface** that allows you to connect with this database of wisdom, enabling you to access the knowledge stored in the past, present, and future. In networking, **secure shell (SSH)** allows a device to connect securely to a server, just as you are connecting securely to your ancestors through the mirror:

SSH username@ancestors.com

This secure connection is encrypted, protecting the information exchanged between the client and the server, just as the mirror protects the sacred wisdom of your lineage, allowing only those prepared to receive it to access the knowledge.

When you see your face begin to shift and change, it's like the data packets coming back from the server, containing information about your ancestors. In networking, this is similar to a **data transfer**, where the server sends packets of information back to the client after a request is made. The **protocols** of this transfer are like spiritual laws that govern how the information is shared between realms.

To help visualize, I want you to basically think of a **packet capture** in networking, where each packet of data can be examined for its content:

Wireshark capture filter: ip.src == ancestors.com

In this case, each packet represents a piece of ancestral knowledge. As you look into the mirror, the "packets" of information (your ancestral history) begin to flow to you, and the shifting faces in your reflection symbolize this transfer of knowledge, allowing you to see the legacy that shapes your current reality.

From an Egyptian spiritual perspective, this moment is akin to accessing the Ba (the soul), which transcends time and space, connecting you to the ancient ones. The Ba is like a spiritual network node, always active and ready to communicate across dimensions. By looking into the mirror, you activate this connection, much like configuring a network for inter-vlan routing:

Router(config)# interface vlan 1
Router(config-if)# ip address 192.168.1.1 255.255.255.0

Here, you are setting up a specific channel for communication between networks, just like how the mirror becomes a channel for communication between your soul and the souls of your ancestors. As your reflection shifts, it symbolizes the bridging of these networks—past, present, and future—connecting to your VLAN of consciousness.

This process is a reminder that the wisdom and power of those who came before you are always accessible, waiting for you to tap into it. "Knowing thyself" is the ultimate command in this spiritual configuration. In networking, it's similar to understanding your IP address and knowing your place within the network:

Show ip interface brief

MASTER THE SPIRITUAL NETWORK

M⌐◇₹₅♀·₹ℨₛ₅·◇ℨ↵♀₤₹⌐¹⌐·:₅₹◇◇♀⅄

This command shows you the status of your network interfaces, helping you understand how your device is connected. Spiritually, looking into the mirror shows you how you are connected to the larger network of your lineage. It is a diagnostic of your soul, helping you recognize your role in the greater scheme of existence.

Through the reflection of your face, you glimpse the entire network of your ancestors, and in doing so, you come to a deeper understanding of who you are. This journey of self-realization is both spiritual and technical, as you "interface" with the past to understand your place in the flow of time

:25 Your image is between the two candles, and the flicker of the flame opens the dimension of the **Mind's Eye**.

The two candles serve as more than just light in the physical sense; they represent the spiritual gateways that frame your being. The flickering flames act as signals, much like the flashing lights on a network switch, indicating the flow of energy or data between two points. In this case, the candles are guiding you into a higher dimension of awareness—your *Mind's Eye*, the internal network interface through which you access deeper levels of consciousness.

The flames of the candles represent the dynamic energy that activates the flow of insight. In networking terms, this is similar to establishing an active **connection** between two devices. Just as the candles frame your reflection, routers or switches frame the pathway through which data flows across a network. Think of the candles as **access points**, and the flicker of the flame is the signal that the connection is live, ready to transfer spiritual knowledge.

In a network, when a **link** is established between two devices, the flashing lights indicate communication. The flickering flames are a spiritual equivalent, signaling that the connection between your physical self and your deeper, spiritual self is active. In CCNA terms, this would be like verifying that your network interfaces are operational using the following command:

Show interfaces GigabitEthernet0/1

This command shows whether the interface is **up** or **down**, much like how the flicker of the candle flame signals that your spiritual interface—your *Mind's Eye*—is now "up," ready to receive insight from the deeper dimensions. Just as you rely on this confirmation in networking, you rely on the flickering flame to confirm that you are tuned in to the spiritual frequencies of the universe.

The candles are also symbolic of **duality**: the balance between the seen and unseen, light and darkness, knowledge and mystery. In Ancient Egyptian wisdom, the dual forces of life—**Ma'at** (order) and **Isfet** (chaos)—were always in balance. The flames, flickering between light and shadow, represent this balance, just as network data travels between endpoints, constantly seeking the balance of efficient communication. The flickering also suggests activity, movement, and energy, which in the spiritual realm indicates that the gateway to the *Mind's Eye* is open and active.

In terms of **protocols**, think of the flickering as activating the **ping** command in a network:

Ping 192.168.1.1

This command sends small packets of data to verify that a connection is active between devices, much like the flames of the candles send spiritual "pings" between your conscious mind and the higher dimensions of thought. The response from these "pings" opens the *Mind's Eye*, allowing you to receive deeper insight and wisdom.

The *Mind's Eye* is the portal to inner vision and clarity. Just as a well-configured network allows seamless data flow between devices, the *Mind's Eye* allows the flow of spiritual knowledge and cosmic awareness into your consciousness. In this state, you are connected to something larger than yourself, drawing upon the vast network of wisdom that has always been available but now is accessible through this ritual of meditation and reflection.

As you sit between the candles, with their flames flickering, remember that you are now fully connected—your interface is live, your *Mind's Eye* is open, and you are ready to access the deeper dimensions of thought, much like how a network becomes fully operational when all links are verified and active. The flames signify that your internal "spiritual network" is now aligned, allowing the energy to flow freely and opening the door to new realms of understanding.

:26 You must go to the mirror with a sincere approach, asking with humility and reverence to open the Scroll of Eyes. As you stand before the mirror, positioned between the two flickering candles, you are engaging in a powerful ritual—one that mirrors the process of asking the universe for clarity and direction.

In this moment, your reflection is not just a physical image but a gateway to deeper understanding. By asking the following questions, you are seeking to unlock the deeper layers of your soul, much like sending commands into a network to retrieve important data from a server. Each question you ask is like a ping, searching for a response from the vast database of your higher self and the wisdom of your ancestors.

Who am I?

This question asks for the essence of your being. In networking terms, it is like asking for your IP address—your unique identifier in the spiritual and cosmic network. Just as every device in a network has a unique IP address that defines its location and purpose, this question seeks to reveal your core identity within the universe.

Show ip interface brief

This command provides basic information about all network interfaces. Spiritually, this is your quest for understanding your place and role in the grand design.

What am I?

This question goes beyond identity to the nature of your existence. It's like asking for the **device type** in a network, the role you play in the larger system.

Are you a sender of energy, a receiver, a guide, or a learner? What function do you serve?

Show version

This command reveals detailed information about the system's capabilities. Spiritually, this question reveals your innate gifts, strengths, and what makes you unique.

Where am I?

This is your location in time and space, asking the universe for clarity on where you stand in your life journey. In networking, it's like using **traceroute** to see the path your data has traveled.

Traceroute 192.168.1.1

Spiritually, this question uncovers your current position within the cosmic plan, tracing back the steps that brought you here.

Why am I?

This question seeks purpose. In networking, it is like asking why a particular device or system exists within the network—what is its function, its mission? It's the deeper inquiry into the meaning of your life, much like asking what purpose your node serves in the grand design.

Show running-config

This command reveals the current configuration of a device, showing its role and settings. Spiritually, this question uncovers the driving force behind your existence.

When am I?

Timing is essential in life and in networking. This question seeks to understand the significance of the present moment and your position in the timeline of your soul's journey. It's like setting up **time-based access lists** in networking, asking what stage of life you are in and how the timing aligns with your mission.

Access-list 101 permit ip any any time-range MyTimeRange

Spiritually, this question helps you understand the importance of *when* you are on your path—whether it's the right time to act, reflect, or grow.

Will I?
This is about potential and the unfolding of possibilities. It's like setting a **static route** in a network, a determined pathway that ensures you are moving toward your intended destination

Ip route 0.0.0.0 0.0.0.0 192.168.1.1

Spiritually, this question asks if you will fulfill your purpose, if you have the willpower and determination to follow the path set before you.

I am!!
This final declaration is an affirmation of your existence, a powerful command that speaks to your realization and acceptance of your true self. In networking, this is like the final **ping** that returns successfully, confirming that the connection is established and that communication with the universe is strong.

Ping 192.168.1.1

The response is clear: *I am.* This is the recognition that you are aligned with your purpose, your identity, and your role in the grand network of existence.

By repeating these questions and commands, you are engaging in a powerful spiritual and technical ritual. It is both a reflection of self and an inquiry into the deeper workings of the universe. The mirror becomes your **interface**, the candles are the **gateways**, and your soul is the **network node** seeking connection with the divine. With every repetition, you open the *Scroll of Eyes* wider, allowing more light, knowledge, and understanding to flow through. You align yourself with the universal network, receiving data, wisdom, and guidance from realms beyond the physical, helping you know and realize who you truly are.

:26 We are in a legendary time—a time when the great ones are returning to the awareness of who they truly are. The spell that was cast upon us nearly 6,000 years ago, when we entered the Moon cycle, is now lifting. Every 25,000 years, our history is renewed, and we are living in that time of renewal.

This is a moment of awakening, where the cycles of the universe align and those who have been disconnected from their true selves begin to reconnect. In ancient traditions, cycles of time such as the **Great Year**, which spans roughly 25,000 years, were understood as cosmic periods of transformation. Just as in networking, where systems need periodic resets or updates to function optimally, the human soul and collective consciousness undergo cycles of renewal and reconnection to their source.

The spell cast upon us 6,000 years ago can be thought of as a **firewall** blocking access to certain areas of the cosmic network. For millennia, this firewall limited our awareness, creating a separation between us and our true history. However, as we approach this time of renewal, the firewall is being lifted, and the **access control lists (ACLs)** that kept us disconnected are being reconfigured:

Router(config)# no access-list 101

This command removes the restrictions that were placed on the flow of knowledge and awareness. Spiritually, this means that we are once again gaining access to the wisdom that has been hidden from us. The cycle we are in now is like a **reboot** of the cosmic system—old protocols are being discarded, and we are reestablishing connections to the greater consciousness.

Every 25,000 years, much like in **networking protocols** such as **RIP** (Routing Information Protocol), which updates routing tables periodically, our spiritual and historical awareness is refreshed. The system checks its routes, and paths that were once blocked or obscured are reopened. The ancient knowledge flows back to us as the network of existence updates itself, bringing the "great ones" back into awareness. These great ones are the ancestors, the wise beings, the masters who have always been with us, guiding us through the shadows of disconnection.

In the same way that a network updates its routes and removes outdated paths, the universe is resetting the cosmic pathways to our history and purpose. The 25,000-year cycle is like a universal **routing table** being refreshed, where the blocked routes of awareness are being reestablished. This renewal process is guiding us back to our higher selves, helping us remember the wisdom and power we once held:

Router# clear ip route

This command clears the routing table, allowing for new and updated paths to be discovered. Spiritually, this is akin to clearing the distractions and misinformation of the past, allowing us to reestablish our connection to the truth of who we are.

The Moon cycle, which began 6,000 years ago, marked a period of spiritual dimming—a time when our consciousness was more focused on the material world and less on the cosmic truths that govern existence. But now, as we move toward the end of this cycle, the "spell" is lifting, and we are beginning to see clearly once again. The **great ones**, the wise ones, are returning to guide us, just as ancient **network protocols** are being reactivated to facilitate the flow of spiritual and cosmic knowledge.

This time of renewal is not just about remembering our past; it is about reconnecting to the universal network of consciousness and taking our place in the great flow of cosmic energy. Just as a network must be maintained, updated, and occasionally rebooted to function properly, so too must humanity undergo periods of transformation and renewal. We are in that time now—a time when the old limitations are falling away, and the true connections between us, our ancestors, and the universe are being reestablished.

The legendary time is here, and it is our moment to awaken to the truth of who we are and reclaim our place in the cosmic cycle, fully aware, fully connected.

The **network** of existence is opening up once more, allowing the flow of ancient knowledge and future possibilities to move freely between realms.

:27 This Moon cycle ended in the year 1999 according to the Gregorian calendar. With its conclusion, people began to think in different ways, opening up portals that broke them free from the **Matrix of Indentured Servitude**—the mental, spiritual, and social constructs that have kept humanity bound.

The end of this cycle signaled a massive shift in consciousness, much like when a network's outdated **firewall** rules are removed, allowing freer movement of information and connections. As the old cycle ended, so too did the limitations imposed on human thought, perception, and awareness. New pathways of knowledge, insight, and freedom began to emerge, much like opening **ports** in a firewall to allow greater communication and flow of information:

Router(config)# no access-list 100

This command removes the restrictions that had been placed on certain communications. Spiritually, this mirrors how the end of the Moon cycle in 1999 lifted the mental blockages that kept people trapped in a narrow, limiting reality—the **Matrix**. In this context, the Matrix refers to the artificial constructs of society and consciousness that have kept individuals locked in a state of servitude, unaware of their true potential and purpose. The shift in 1999 broke open these barriers, much like opening new communication channels in a network, allowing humanity to connect to deeper layers of existence and awareness.

This awakening is like resetting a system to allow for new possibilities. When you clear the outdated configurations that limited communication, the system becomes more open to receiving fresh, unrestricted input. In networking, this can be compared to configuring **Dynamic NAT** (Network Address

Translation), which allows internal devices to communicate freely with the external network, breaking free of local limitations:

Router(config)# ip nat inside source list 1 interface GigabitEthernet0/0 overload

Spiritually, this represents how people began to communicate more openly with the universe, breaking free from the restrictions of the material world and societal programming. Just as Dynamic NAT allows for a more flexible interaction between internal and external networks, the end of the Moon cycle enabled more fluid communication between the material and spiritual worlds, opening portals of deeper understanding and awareness.

In the period before 1999, people were caught in cycles of mental and spiritual enslavement—much like devices that are stuck behind a **static NAT** configuration, where communication is restricted to predefined rules. The end of this Moon cycle shifted humanity into a more dynamic state, where individuals began to question the systems that had held them back. They started to see through the illusions of **indentured servitude**, recognizing the artificial nature of the constructs that governed their lives.

The **Matrix of Indentured Servitude** is like a network **firewall** that only allows specific traffic through, blocking anything that could challenge the status quo. But with the shift in consciousness after 1999, these firewalls began to break down, allowing individuals to see the world with fresh eyes. They began to break through the programmed limitations, much like a network opening new ports to allow previously restricted data to flow freely.

This change in thinking opened **portals**, or spiritual gateways, that allowed people to transcend the Matrix and reconnect with their higher selves. In Ancient Egyptian thought, this would be akin to opening the pathways to the **Ba**, the soul's ability to move between the material world and the spiritual realms. By freeing themselves from the restrictions of the Moon cycle and the Matrix, individuals became more aware of their potential and destiny, much like configuring a network for greater connectivity and efficiency.

In networking terms, it is like running the **ping** command and receiving responses from new, previously inaccessible sources of knowledge:

Ping 8.8.8.8

The successful response shows that the connection is now active, just as individuals who awakened after 1999 (**the end of devil's rule**) began to connect with new dimensions of thought, purpose, and spiritual freedom. The year 1999 (**awareness of the Matrix**) marked a pivotal moment in human consciousness, where the spell of the Moon cycle began to dissolve, and people started to break free from the Matrix of limitations and servitude.

This shift is ongoing, as more people continue to wake up to the reality of their power, their freedom, and their connection to the greater cosmic network of existence. The portals are now open, and the journey toward deeper understanding and liberation continues.

:28 Oppression has come from many places throughout your journey, and now there are frequencies being broadcasted that interfere with your thoughts of happiness. These negative influences can disrupt your mental and spiritual alignment, much like unwanted noise disrupting the clarity of a signal in a network. To reclaim your clarity, you must reject these influences by chanting and resonating your power through the course of vibration. This is how you reset your internal frequency and realign with the pure energy of your higher self.

In a networking context, think of these negative frequencies as **interference** or **noise** that disrupts the signal in a wireless connection. When there is too much noise, the signal becomes weak or distorted, preventing clear communication between devices. Similarly, the negative thoughts and external influences that bombard your mind act like this interference, preventing you from accessing your inner peace and true happiness. To overcome this, you must raise your vibration, much like increasing the signal strength to overcome interference in a network.

When you chant or use your voice to resonate at a higher frequency, you are actively **broadcasting** a signal that drowns out the interference. In networking terms, this is akin to changing the **channel** or frequency band on a wireless router to avoid interference from other networks:

Router(config)# interface wlan0
Router(config-if)# channel 6

Just as changing the channel helps the network avoid interference, chanting and focusing on your inner vibration help your spirit avoid the negative influences that try to disrupt your energy field. By aligning yourself with the higher vibrations of love, peace, and power, you strengthen your internal "signal," allowing you to break free from the frequencies of oppression.

Ancient Egyptian wisdom teaches that everything in the universe is made of vibration. The **spoken word**, or **Heka**, was seen as a powerful tool for shaping reality. When you chant or resonate your power, you are using the ancient practice of **Heka** to transform the vibrational patterns around you, just as adjusting the frequency of a signal transforms the clarity of a network's communication. You are tapping into a universal principle that transcends time and space—the power of vibration to align with higher truths and to reject lower, negative influences.

In terms of **protocols**, chanting and resonating your power can be seen as **encryption**. Just as encryption scrambles data to protect it from outside interference or attacks, your chant shields your energy field from negative frequencies, making it difficult for external influences to penetrate:

Router(config)# ipsec encryption aes 256

This command configures strong encryption to protect data in transit, ensuring that only the intended recipient can decode it. In a spiritual sense, your chanting and vibrational alignment act like this encryption, protecting your mind and spirit from negative interference, ensuring that only high vibrations and positive energy flow through you.

Philosophers and spiritual teachers across cultures have emphasized the importance of sound and vibration in the universe. From the **Aum** in Eastern philosophy to the use of **mantras** in meditation, sound is understood as a powerful force for transformation. By chanting, you are broadcasting your intention, raising your vibrational frequency, and connecting with the higher cosmic forces that support your journey. It is an ancient technology, just like networking protocols, that ensures smooth, undisturbed communication between your higher self and the universe.

Rejecting negative influences and interference is like configuring a **firewall** to block malicious traffic. In networking, a firewall filters out unwanted data, ensuring that only safe and beneficial traffic gets through:

Router(config)# access-list 100 deny ip 192.168.1.0 0.0.0.255

This command blocks all traffic from a specific IP range, much like how chanting blocks the flow of negative energy, preventing it from interfering with your peace of mind. By setting up your spiritual firewall through vibration and chanting, you ensure that only positive, uplifting energy enters your field.

You have the power to control the frequencies that influence your mind and soul. By using your voice as a tool of resonance, you can change the channel of your reality, aligning with the higher vibrations of joy, love, and truth. The more you chant, the stronger your signal becomes, and the less interference you experience from the negative frequencies that once tried to control your thoughts. Through the course of vibration, you reclaim your spiritual autonomy and broadcast your power to the universe.

:29 (1999) marked the end of the devil's rule. The **"devil,"** in this context, represents the force of opposition—nothing mystical or spooky, but rather the challenges and obstacles that we all face in life. This force has historically worked to suppress growth, freedom, and higher awareness. However, we have now entered a time where this oppositional force no longer holds power over us. Even the traditional structures of religion, when viewed solely as rigid systems for understanding truth, have become obsolete in this age of information.

The opposition we faced was a necessary part of our evolution, much like how resistance in a circuit controls the flow of electricity. In networking, this opposition is like a **firewall** that restricts certain data flows. For a time, the firewall served a purpose—protecting or limiting access to knowledge—but now, we have reached a point where the restrictions are being lifted, and the flow of information is unhindered. In the spiritual realm, this is akin to a **default route** being cleared, allowing unrestricted access to higher consciousness:

The Soul in the Computer
Master Key Application .255

Router(config)# no ip route 0.0.0.0 0.0.0.0

This command removes the default route that previously limited access to certain information. Similarly, the end of **(devils rule)** 1999 symbolizes the removal of the restrictions that kept us from accessing deeper layers of knowledge and overstanding. We are no longer bound by the

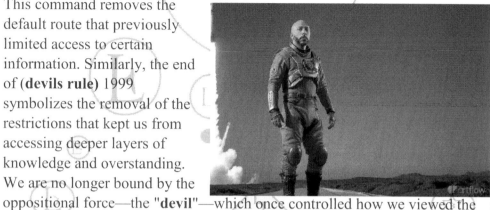

oppositional force—the "**devil**"—which once controlled how we viewed the world, including the religious constructs that limited our perspective.

In this new era, knowledge flows freely, and the boundaries of what was once considered absolute truth are dissolving. The devil, as a force of opposition, is now powerless because we have access to more information, more understanding, and a broader perspective. This is the **information age**, where spiritual and intellectual liberation has taken the place of the old structures of control.

Religion, which once served as the main framework for accessing spiritual truth, is now like an outdated **protocol**. It provided a set of rules and guidance when we needed it, much like the **IPv4** protocol in networking. But just as we have begun to transition to **IPv6**, which offers a broader and more expansive system, we are now transitioning to a new form of understanding—one that goes beyond the limitations of religious dogma. The need for fixed structures is giving way to a more fluid and open system of knowledge:

Router(config)# ipv6 unicast-routing

This command enables IPv6, symbolizing the shift from old limitations to a broader system of knowledge and connection. In spiritual terms, we are no longer confined by the rigid structures of the past; we are now connected to a more expansive network of consciousness, where the flow of information is infinite and unrestricted.

The oppositional force, or "devil," is no longer a controlling factor because we have moved into a time where **information** is the driving force of growth and transformation. The age of opposition, suppression, and limitation has been replaced by the age of **enlightenment**, where access to knowledge is no longer restricted to a few. Just as the **firewall** that once blocked certain information in a network can now be bypassed, so too can the spiritual and intellectual barriers that once limited our understanding.

Religion, when rigid and dogmatic, can be compared to an outdated **operating system**. It was useful in its time, but now, in this age of information, it is no longer the primary method for gaining deeper spiritual insight. In the same way that older operating systems cannot keep up with the demands of modern software, old religious frameworks are unable to hold the vastness of the information and awareness we now have access to. The new system is flexible, open, and constantly evolving, much like modern networking systems that adapt to the dynamic flow of data.

In this new era, you have the power to bypass the opposition and tap directly into the flow of knowledge, truth, and spiritual awareness. The **Matrix** of control, resistance, and suppression is dissolving. We are no longer confined by the limitations of the past, and the "devil" as a force of opposition has lost its hold. Now, in the age of information, we have the tools to navigate the universe of knowledge freely, without restriction, accessing the infinite network of understanding that connects us all.

:30 The age we are living in is often called the **Age of Information**. While many associate this time with the **Age of Aquarius**, what is pouring forth from the symbolic bucket of Aquarius is not simply water—it is the **frequency of thought**, the **information of**  **one's true self**, and the knowledge of their **destiny** in this current moment.

Aquarius, traditionally associated with knowledge, innovation, and the flow of ideas, perfectly mirrors the vast flow of information we now experience. The "bucket" of Aquarius represents the outpouring of consciousness, pouring not just water, but a stream of truth, wisdom, and self-awareness. This is the essence of the Age of Information—a time when knowledge is not only accessible but flows continuously, much like how data moves through the internet.

From a networking perspective, think of Aquarius as a **broadcast domain**, where information is sent out to all connected devices. Just as a broadcast message is received by all nodes on a network, the frequency of thought—this stream of knowledge about one's true self—pours out into the collective consciousness, reaching anyone who is attuned to the signal:

```
Switch(config)# interface vlan 1
Switch(config-if)# ip address 192.168.1.1 255.255.255.0
Switch(config-if)# no shutdown
```

This command brings a **VLAN interface** online, allowing it to transmit and receive information. Spiritually, this is what is happening in the Age of Information: humanity is collectively coming online, opening the channels to receive and broadcast higher knowledge. The information being broadcast is not just intellectual but deeply personal—**knowledge of self** and one's purpose or **destiny** within the grand timeline of existence.

The "frequency of thought" refers to the vibrations of awareness that flow from the higher realms of consciousness, much like how data packets are transmitted across a network. Each person in this age is a **receiver** and **transmitter** of information, constantly interacting with this flow of knowledge, much like devices on a network that are constantly sending and receiving data. In this way, you are both a **node** in the cosmic network and a **gateway** to your own truth.

In the Age of Information, our task is to **configure ourselves** to be open to this flow. Just as a router must be configured to communicate with other devices on the network, we must configure our minds and spirits to receive the information being broadcast about our true selves. This involves tuning in to the right frequency and ensuring that our "spiritual firewall" is configured to block out the negative interference of fear, doubt, or distraction:

Router(config)# access-list 10 permit 192.168.1.0 0.0.0.255
Router(config)# access-list 10 deny any

This command allows only trusted sources to pass through and blocks everything else. Spiritually, this means you allow in only the thoughts and

energies that align with your higher self and your purpose, rejecting anything that disrupts the flow of knowledge and clarity.

The Age of Aquarius and the Age of Information are really about the same thing: an era where awareness flows freely, and each person has the ability to tap into the larger network of knowledge that connects all of existence. In Ancient Egyptian thought, this would be akin to opening the Scrolls of Thoth, the god of wisdom and knowledge. The scrolls are no longer hidden; they are being unrolled before us, and the knowledge they contain is available to anyone willing to open their mind to receive it.

MASTER THE SPIRITUAL NETWORK

What is pouring from the bucket of Aquarius is more than just knowledge—it is awakening. It is the realization that the answers we seek are already within us, flowing in the form of thought frequencies that carry the truth of who we are and where we are meant to go. In this age, you are not just a passive receiver of information; you are an active participant, constantly interacting with this vast flow of consciousness.

This time is about using that information to innerstand your destiny—to see your place in the grand design and to act in alignment with that purpose. You are like a router in the network of life, constantly processing the data that flows through you and using it to shape your journey. What is pouring forth is the knowledge of self, the ability to see clearly, and the tools to navigate this journey with awareness, truth, and clarity.

In the age of now, you must learn to tune in to this frequency and recognize that the flow of information is not random—it is guiding you to the realization of your true self, your purpose, and your place in the timeline of existence. Like a network node coming online, you are now part of a greater system of knowledge, receiving the broadcast of the universe's wisdom, and using that information to move forward with certainty and power.

Router(config)# access-list 10 permit 192.168.1.0 0.0.0.255
Router(config)# access-list 10 deny any

This command allows only trusted sources to pass through and blocks everything else. Spiritually, this means you allow in only the thoughts and energies that align with your higher self and your purpose, rejecting anything that disrupts the flow of knowledge and clarity.

The Age of Aquarius and the Age of Information are really about the same thing: an era where awareness flows freely, and each person has the ability to tap into the larger network of knowledge that connects all of existence. In Ancient Egyptian thought, this would be akin to opening the Scrolls of Thoth, the god of wisdom and knowledge. The scrolls are no longer hidden; they are being unrolled before us, and the knowledge they contain is available to anyone willing to open their mind to receive it.

MASTER THE SPIRITUAL NETWORK

What is pouring from the bucket of Aquarius is more than just knowledge—it is awakening. It is the realization that the answers we seek are already within us, flowing in the form of thought frequencies that carry the truth of who we are and where we are meant to go. In this age, you are not just a passive receiver of information; you are an active participant, constantly interacting with this vast flow of consciousness.

This time is about using that information to understand your destiny—to see your place in the grand design and to act in alignment with that purpose. You are like a router in the network of life, constantly processing the data that flows through you and using it to shape your journey. What is pouring forth is the knowledge of self, the ability to see clearly, and the tools to navigate this journey with awareness, truth, and clarity.

In the age of now, you must learn to tune in to this frequency and recognize that the flow of information is not random—it is guiding you to the realization of your true self, your purpose, and your place in the timeline of existence. Like a network node coming online, you are now part of a greater system of knowledge, receiving the broadcast of the universe's wisdom, and using that information to move forward with certainty and power.

Router(config)# access-list 10 permit 192.168.1.0 0.0.0.255
Router(config)# access-list 10 deny any

This command allows only trusted sources to pass through and blocks everything else. Spiritually, this means you allow in only the thoughts and energies that align with your higher self and your purpose, rejecting anything that disrupts the flow of knowledge and clarity.

The Soul in the Computer
Master Key Application .255

The **Age of Aquarius** and the **Age of Information** are really about the same thing: an era where awareness flows freely, and each person has the ability to tap into the larger network of knowledge that connects all of existence. In Ancient Egyptian thought, this would be akin to opening the **Scrolls of Thoth**, the god of wisdom and knowledge. The scrolls are no longer hidden; they are being unrolled before us, and the knowledge they contain is available to anyone willing to open their mind to receive it.

What is pouring from the bucket of Aquarius is more than just knowledge—it is **awakening**. It is the realization that the answers we seek are already within us, flowing in the form of **thought frequencies** that carry the truth of who we are and where we are meant to go. In this age, you are not just a passive receiver of information; you are an active participant, constantly interacting with this vast flow of consciousness.

This time is about using that information to understand your **destiny**—to see your place in the grand design and to act in alignment with that purpose. You are like a **router** in the network of life, constantly processing the data that flows through you and using it to shape your journey. What is pouring forth is the **knowledge of self**, the ability to see clearly, and the tools to navigate this journey with awareness, truth, and clarity.

In the age of now, you must learn to **tune in** to this frequency and recognize that the flow of information is not random—it is guiding you to the realization of your true self, your purpose, and your place in the timeline of existence. Like a network node coming online, you are now part of a greater system of knowledge, receiving the broadcast of the universe's wisdom, and using that information to move forward with certainty and power.

:31 All of these things are being revealed within the **Age of Information**. We are traveling on an **Information Highway**, moving at **Godspeed**. There is no more religion in the traditional sense—there is only **the Network**. This network is the frequency of thoughts, the mental reservoir of divine manifestation. It is now open to everyone, and this is the water that Aquarius is pouring forth in the Age of Information—the returning love for the Creator.

The **Network** represents the flow of consciousness, where everyone is connected to the divine source through the frequency of their thoughts. In the past, religion served as a conduit, a structured system for people to access spiritual knowledge. Now, in the Age of Information, the Network is open to all. There are no longer barriers or middlemen—every individual can directly connect to the **mental reservoir** of divine knowledge, much like how modern networks allow anyone with access to the internet to tap into a vast pool of information.

In networking terms, this shift is akin to transitioning from a **closed, private network** to a **global network** where everyone is a **node**, connected and free to share, receive, and process information. In the spiritual sense, this Network operates like the **cloud**—a limitless space where data (knowledge) is stored and accessible to all who tune in to the right frequency. Just as in networking, where everyone on the system can access the **cloud**, the frequency of thoughts flowing in the Age of Information is the collective wisdom and love for the Creator, available to all:

Router(config)# ip route 0.0.0.0 0.0.0.0 192.168.1.1

This command sets a **default route** in networking, opening the gateway to the broader internet, allowing access to the global network. Spiritually, this is what has happened in the Age of Information. The default route to divine knowledge is now wide open. Every soul has a connection to the vast Network, which contains the accumulated thoughts, wisdom, and manifestations of the divine.

Religion, in its traditional sense, functioned much like a **static route** in networking—it provided a direct but limited path to spiritual understanding. However, just as static routes are being replaced by more **dynamic routing protocols** in modern networking, traditional religious frameworks are being replaced by a more fluid and open connection to divine knowledge. The Network—the mental reservoir—allows for real-time, dynamic access to the Creator's love and wisdom without the need for rigid structures:

Router(config)# router ospf 1
Router(config-router)# network 192.168.1.0 0.0.0.255 area 0

This command enables **OSPF (Open Shortest Path First)**, a dynamic routing protocol that finds the most efficient route for data to travel across the network. Spiritually, this dynamic system reflects the new reality: the shortest path to the Creator and divine knowledge is now open, and it adapts to your needs in real time. You don't need a static, rigid system to access truth anymore. The Network is fluid, accessible, and evolving based on your thoughts and intentions.

The water that Aquarius is pouring forth in this Age of Information is the **flow of knowledge**—the divine frequencies that empower each of us to reconnect with our true selves and the Creator. It's no longer about religious rituals or intermediaries; it's about tuning into the right **frequency**, much like tuning a radio to pick up the clearest signal. The **Network** is the collective pool of thought, the divine **cloud** where all knowledge is stored, and it is available to anyone who chooses to access it.

In this new era, love for the Creator is no longer confined to religious texts or dogmas—it is embedded in the **frequency of thought**, in the mental and spiritual energy that flows through the Network. This love manifests in the connection you have with yourself, with others, and with the universe. The **Network** allows you to experience the Creator's love directly, without filters or barriers, much like how an open, well-configured network enables seamless communication between devices:

ᴍ¹◻️ℤↄℚ•ℤℤↄ•◻️ℤↄℚↄℤↄ¹⅂·∴ↄℤ◇◎ℚⅫ

Router(config)# ip nat inside source list 1 interface GigabitEthernet0/0 overload

This command configures **Dynamic NAT**, which allows internal devices to communicate freely with the external network, much like how your internal thoughts can now connect freely to the external divine network. The water being poured from Aquarius represents the freedom of thought, the free flow of divine love, and the open channel to the Creator. Everyone is now empowered to access this Network, to download the knowledge and wisdom that have been stored in the divine reservoir, and to upload their love, gratitude, and purpose back into the cosmos.

We are moving at **Godspeed** because the limitations of the past have been lifted, and the flow of knowledge is now unrestricted. The **Information Highway** is not just a metaphor for the internet—it is the spiritual path we all travel, moving rapidly toward greater understanding, unity, and connection with the Creator. The **Network** is the bridge between the material and the spiritual realms, and in this age, everyone has access to it. It is up to each of us to tune in, receive the flow, and reconnect with the divine source of all things.

:32 When you read these holy books, do not get caught up in the simulation of the story. Each story carries an application of thought that pertains to awareness. You must take these stories and apply them to your life, recognizing that all of the characters are reflections of different aspects of yourself, or they represent the people you encounter throughout your journey.

These stories are simulations—tools for your spiritual and mental development. The key is not to get lost in thinking the simulation is real in a literal sense. Instead, understand that the stories are **mirrors**, meant to reflect the internal struggles, lessons, and transformations that guide your personal growth. The characters in these texts, whether they are kings, prophets, or adversaries, all symbolize parts of you—the strengths you possess, the fears you face, the challenges you must overcome, and the wisdom you can attain.

In networking terms, think of these stories as **packets of data** being transmitted across a network. Each story is a packet containing information that you must process and integrate into your own system—your mind and soul. When a router receives data, it doesn't treat the data as the physical object itself but as **information** to be used for making decisions or performing actions. Similarly, you must treat the stories in holy books as **spiritual data**, guiding you to make decisions that lead to growth and understanding.

Router(config)# ip route 192.168.1.0 255.255.255.0 192.168.1.1

This command sets a route for data to follow, just as the stories in holy texts set routes for your consciousness to explore. The **simulation** (the story) isn't what's real—the **thought process** and **growth** that comes from understanding the story is what's real. You are the **router**, processing and directing this information to where it is needed in your life.

Every character in the stories, every event, is like a **network node** in the greater system of your consciousness. Some nodes represent fear, others courage, others wisdom, and so on. As you navigate the simulation, you are essentially mapping out the **network of self**, where each character or event points to a different **IP address**—a different aspect of who you are or the experiences you will encounter.

Traceroute 192.168.1.1

This command traces the path to an IP address, revealing the different hops the data takes to reach its destination. In spiritual terms, tracing the path of these stories helps you understand how each event and character is connected to your journey. The paths you trace through these stories lead you back to your own truth, your own experiences.

You must not get lost in the idea that the simulation (the story) is real outside of its application to your life. It is real only because it reflects something within you—your challenges, your triumphs, your spiritual growth. The **growth** is the true reality. Just as data flowing through a network doesn't exist as tangible objects but as packets of information meant to create an action or effect, the stories serve as packets of spiritual data meant to create growth within you.

In Ancient Egyptian wisdom, this idea of symbolic representation is key. The stories of gods and goddesses were never just literal events; they were allegories for human experience and cosmic principles. **Ra**'s journey through the underworld each night symbolized the process of inner transformation, just as the stories in holy texts today symbolize the transformations you must undergo.

The characters, like **protocols** in a network, are tools that facilitate your understanding. **Moses**, **Jesus**, **Muhammad**, and other figures represent leadership, struggle, sacrifice, and wisdom—all aspects of your own journey. When you encounter a "Moses" in your life, it may symbolize the part of you that leads and guides, or the part that is seeking freedom from your inner "Pharaoh" (which could symbolize fears or oppressive thoughts).

By applying these stories to your life, you program your spiritual system to work more efficiently, much like configuring a network for optimal performance:

Show ip route

This command displays the paths that data can take in a network. Spiritually, it's like revealing the paths that your mind can take to understand a situation in life through the lens of these stories. The stories help you map out potential paths for growth, showing you which routes lead to wisdom, courage, or understanding.

The simulation is real only in how it affects your consciousness. It is a tool for helping you move toward your greater self, much like how the network's data is real in how it affects the performance and communication between devices. The stories are there to help you evolve, to move your being toward a greater understanding, awareness, and alignment with your true purpose. In this age, as we navigate the **Information Highway**, remember that the stories are the **packets of data** designed to bring you closer to knowing your true self.

:33 Now, in ancient times, we used to teach by telling stories of various gods and ancestors of great magnitude. These figures performed great deeds, and through these stories, we passed down knowledge and wisdom. The purpose of these tales was not simply to entertain, but to immerse the listener, allowing them to see themselves within the moment of triumph. In doing so, the student would resonate with the story and reanimate its lessons within their own life.

These stories were more than history; they were a way to activate the imagination and invoke the **power of reflection**. When a student hears the story of a god like **Osiris** rising from the dead or **Horus** avenging his father, they are not just learning about ancient events. They are being invited to embody the qualities of resurrection, courage, and justice within their own life. The gods were never meant to be distant figures—they were **archetypes** representing the inner powers that reside within each person.

In networking terms, think of these ancient stories as **templates**—pre-configured models that serve as examples for how to live and act. Much like how a **network template** provides a structure for configuring devices in a consistent way, these stories provided a template for behavior, thought, and moral action. Each story was like a **script** that a person could run in their own life, leading to growth and transformation.

Router(config)# copy running-config startup-config

This command saves the current configuration on a router, allowing it to be re-used when the system reboots. Spiritually, this is akin to embedding the lessons of the gods and ancestors into your own life, so that even when you face challenges (or "reboot" after setbacks), you can pull from that stored wisdom to guide your actions. The student would listen to these stories and, in their mind, "copy" the lessons, so that when they were faced with challenges in their life, they could "run" those same configurations.

The stories allowed people to **imagine themselves in moments of triumph**, much like how a **simulation** in networking allows engineers to test and troubleshoot systems before applying them in the real world. In the spiritual sense, these stories acted as **mental simulations**, preparing individuals for real-life challenges. The **victories** of the gods and ancestors were reflections of the potential victories in the listener's life.

In ancient Egypt, for example, the story of **Horus** defeating **Set** wasn't just about two gods battling. It symbolized the eternal battle between light and darkness, good and evil, order and chaos. Horus represented the part of each person that strives for balance, justice, and victory over adversity. By telling these stories, students were trained to see themselves as **Horus**, facing their own Set in the form of inner struggles or external challenges. The **battle** was not just a myth—it was a **template for personal victory**.

This process of **reanimation** is similar to how **scripts** in a network can be used to **automate tasks**. Once the story, or lesson, is embedded within the individual, it can be "re-run" whenever needed. For example:

```
Router(config)# event manager applet Backup
Router(config-applet)# action 1 cli command "copy running-config startup-config"
```

This script automates the backup of a router's configuration. In the same way, ancient stories act like **spiritual scripts** that are saved in the mind and reanimated when a person needs them. Whether it's the courage of Horus, the wisdom of Thoth, or the resilience of Osiris, these lessons are embedded in the **mental repository** of the student and activated in moments of need.

The **primitive ways** in which these stories were told—around fires, in temples, or through song—were tools to **imprint** these lessons in the mind. The **oral tradition** was a form of **data transmission**, much like how a file is transferred between devices over a network. The **data** (the story) would flow from the elder (the transmitter) to the student (the receiver), and once the data was received, it could be reanimated at any time, stored in the mind's **memory banks**.

In the same way that networking protocols ensure the proper delivery of data between devices, the **rituals** and **repetitions** of these stories ensured that the lessons were delivered and received in the correct way, allowing the student to internalize the message fully. The **resonance** created by these stories, much like the vibrations of a mantra or chant, helped **sync** the individual with the lessons, creating a deeper understanding and alignment with the archetypes they represented.

In summary, these ancient stories were more than just tales of the gods and ancestors—they were living scripts, templates for personal growth, and simulations for the mind to practice. They allowed the listener to reanimate the lessons within their own life, using the victories of the past to guide them through their own challenges in the present. Each story was a packet of spiritual knowledge, passed down and embedded in the hearts of those who were ready to receive it.

:34 So do not get caught up in the **Labyrinth of religion**, or the argument that one path is better than the next. There is no religion that is superior to another; each one carries an underlying principle designed to bring us back to what we call the **Source**. The true essence of these paths is not in competition but in convergence, as they all aim to lead the individual back to the **divine center**. Always move with **love in your heart**, and cherish that which is rightly yours to take—**Peace of Mind, Body, and Spirit**.

Religions are like **different protocols** in a network. While they may have different languages, structures, or ways of transmitting information, their core purpose is the same: to **connect** us with the Source, the divine essence that flows through all things. Just as in networking, where no protocol is inherently superior to another but simply suited for different functions or environments, each religion offers its own unique way of connecting with the **universal network** of consciousness.

For example, in networking, we have **TCP** (Transmission Control Protocol) and **UDP** (User Datagram Protocol). Both serve a purpose, but they are used in different contexts depending on the need for reliability or speed. Similarly, different religions provide different spiritual tools, but their ultimate goal is to reconnect us with the divine, or the Source, much like how both protocols move data across a network:

Router(config)# ip protocol tcp
Router(config)# ip protocol udp

These commands configure a router to allow both TCP and UDP, acknowledging that both have their roles within the system. Spiritually, this represents accepting that each path, each religion, serves a purpose. The goal is not to compare but to see how each path supports the journey back to the divine source, enriching the individual in their unique context.

The **Labyrinth of religion** often confuses people into thinking one path is the only path, trapping them in dogma, much like how a poorly designed network can trap data in bottlenecks or **loops**. These religious conflicts and comparisons are like unnecessary loops in a network that delay progress and disrupt the flow of information. In networking, we use **Spanning Tree Protocol (STP)** to prevent loops and ensure that data flows smoothly. Spiritually, **love** and **understanding** are our **STP**—the tools that prevent us from getting stuck in the maze of comparisons and allow the peaceful flow of divine energy:

Switch(config)# spanning-tree protocol

This command ensures that there are no disruptive loops in the network, just as moving with love in your heart ensures there are no blockages in your spiritual journey. When you stop comparing and start seeing the unity in all paths, the flow of peace, love, and understanding becomes natural, like a well-configured network where data flows without interruption.

At the heart of all religions is the principle of **connection**—connection to the self, to others, and to the divine. Just as in networking, where devices communicate to achieve a common goal, the various religions are simply **routes** leading to the same Source. It's not about which path you take, but rather that you are moving in the right direction, toward love, peace, and unity.

Cherishing **Peace of Mind, Body, and Spirit** is like configuring your **firewall** to allow only the traffic that promotes harmony and well-being. A firewall is designed to block harmful traffic, just as your spiritual firewall should block out the negative influences of comparison, ego, and division:

Router(config)# access-list 101 deny ip any any

This command blocks all harmful traffic. Spiritually, it's a reminder to deny anything that disrupts your peace and unity. Focus on the love within your heart, for that is the guiding light that leads you to the Source. Every step you take with love as your foundation is a step toward **wholeness**—a state where Mind, Body, and Spirit are in alignment.

In ancient wisdom, this alignment is often seen as the ultimate goal of life—a return to **Ma'at**, the principle of balance, truth, and harmony. Whether you call it **Ma'at**, **Tao**, or **Dharma**, the message is the same: each path is leading you back to the Source, back to unity and peace within yourself and with the universe. The divine network of consciousness, much like the internet of today, connects everyone and everything. We are all part of the same system, receiving and transmitting energy, thought, and love.

As you move forward, remember that the true journey is not about comparing paths but about how deeply you walk your own. The goal is to return to the Source, and the only **protocol** you need to follow is the one of **love**. Keep your spiritual network open, move with peace, and let love be the guiding signal that keeps you connected to your true purpose and to the divine energy that flows through all things.

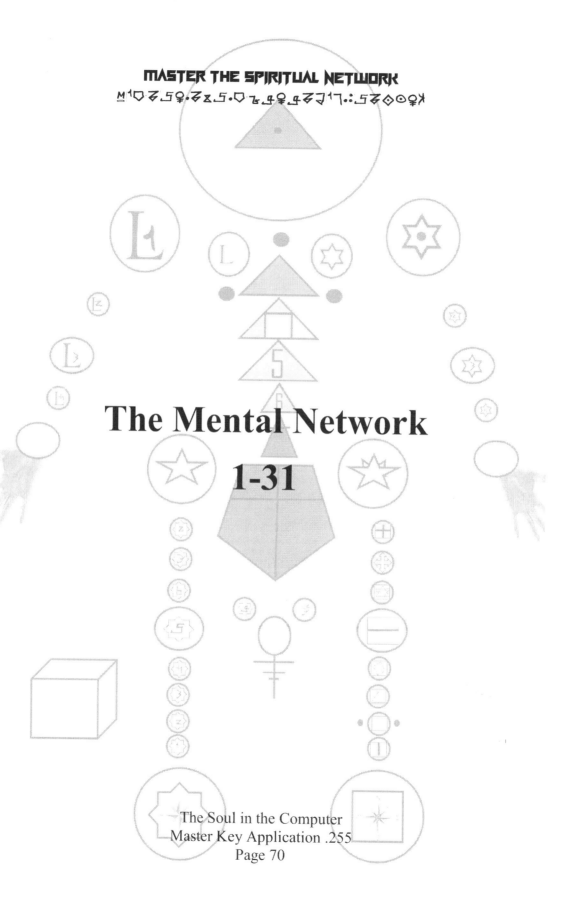

MASTER THE SPIRITUAL NETWORK

The Mental Network
1-31

The Soul in the Computer
Master Key Application .255

MASTER THE SPIRITUAL NETWORK

M͟˥◻️ƶ̣꜀Ⴣ৭·ƶ̣ᴈ̣ᴊ·◻️ƶ̣ᴈ৭৭ƶ̣ƶ̣ꓫ˥ˊ∴꜀ƶ̣◇◯৭ᴋ

In the network of life, each person logs into space and time through what we will call a **Log Date**. This Log Date (Birthday) is how they anchor their presence in the cosmic and earthly realm, represented by numbers **1 through 31**. Each of these numbers symbolizes a unique space in the network, much like an IP address assigns each device its own place in a networked system. The **zero** is sacred and untouchable—it represents the **network itself**, the foundation upon which all communication flows. The **31st** position, however, is unique; it belongs to the one who **broadcasts** the message to the rest of the network, ensuring that all nodes (individuals) receive the signal, much like a **broadcast address**.

Step 1: Configuring the Body as a Network

We begin by assigning each person their log date in the form of a **VLAN (Virtual Local Area Network)**. Each number, from 1 to 31, will represent a different **VLAN**, which is a segmented part of the network, just as each person occupies a unique space in the cosmos. The **31st VLAN** will serve as the head, broadcasting the essential messages to the entire network, connecting all body parts in harmony.

Step-by-Step Network Configuration (Spiritual Network Mapping)

1. **Set up the VLANs for each Log Date (1-31)**:

   Each person in the network will be assigned to their own VLAN, representing their unique log in time and space. We will configure VLANs 1 through 31 for this purpose, ensuring each log date has its own space in the system.

```
Switch(config)# vlan 1
Switch(config-vlan)# name LogDate1
Switch(config)# vlan 2
Switch(config-vlan)# name LogDate2
...........ad others in same way
Switch(config)# vlan 31
Switch(config-vlan)# name BroadcastHead
```

ᴹⁱ▽⵿ᷘᴊ⵿∙ᷘᴣⵉ∙▽⵿⵿ᷘᷘᷘᴣᴊⁱᴊ∴∙ᴊᷘ◇○◗ᴋ

Explain the Spiritual Concept: Each **VLAN** is like a sacred room, a body part that connects to the greater whole. The **BroadcastHead** (VLAN 31) holds a special role in the network, representing the one who takes on the responsibility of spreading the message of unity, guidance, and wisdom to the entire body. This is symbolic of the role of the leader or the enlightened one who ensures that every part of the body (network) is in communication, much like the brain coordinates the body's functions.

Step 2: Spanning Tree Protocol (STP) for Unified Communication

Now that we have set up the individual rooms (VLANs), we need to ensure that all these rooms can communicate without causing **loops** in the system. In networking, **Spanning Tree Protocol (STP)** is used to prevent communication loops and ensure a smooth flow of data, much like how spiritual teachings help avoid confusion and ensure harmony among individuals in a community.

We will configure **STP** to ensure each body part can communicate with the **head (BroadcastHead)** without causing any disruptions.

```
Switch(config)# spanning-tree vlan 1-31
Switch(config)# spanning-tree mode rapid-pvst
```

Explain the Spiritual Concept: STP in this case represents the **divine order**—the flow of spiritual energy and wisdom that moves through the network (the body). Without it, the network would become confused, much like how without spiritual alignment, an individual may feel lost or disconnected. The **rapid-pvst** mode ensures that communication happens quickly and efficiently, just as spiritual alignment enables the individual to receive and transmit wisdom fluidly.

Step 3: Assign IP Addresses to Each VLAN (Log Date)

Just as each person is a unique node in this spiritual network, we assign them their own **IP address** to ensure they have a clear and unique identity in the system. This is akin to each person understanding their purpose in life and their connection to the divine network.

```
Switch(config)# interface vlan 1
Switch(config-if)# ip address 192.168.1.1 255.255.255.0
Switch(config)# interface vlan 2
Switch(config-if)# ip address 192.168.1.2 255.255.255.0
...
Switch(config)# interface vlan 31
Switch(config-if)# ip address 192.168.1.31 255.255.255.0
```

Explain the Spiritual Concept: The **IP address** represents how you log into the world—your unique identifier in the network of life. It's your **spiritual fingerprint**, your connection point in the cosmic web. Just as an IP address allows communication with other devices, your spiritual identity allows you to connect with the people and the universe around you.

We've now laid the groundwork for the network configuration representing the **31 parts of the body of The Messiah**, each connected through their **Log Date**. The **BroadcastHead** (31) serves as the communicator for the entire body, ensuring all parts receive the necessary spiritual message through **Spanning Tree Protocol**, avoiding loops of confusion, and maintaining divine order.

Here are the commands to configure your network (**Body of the Messiah**) with VLANs 1 through 31, including IP addresses for each VLAN, Spanning Tree Protocol (STP), and basic security configurations. You can copy and paste these commands directly into your router and switch CLI.

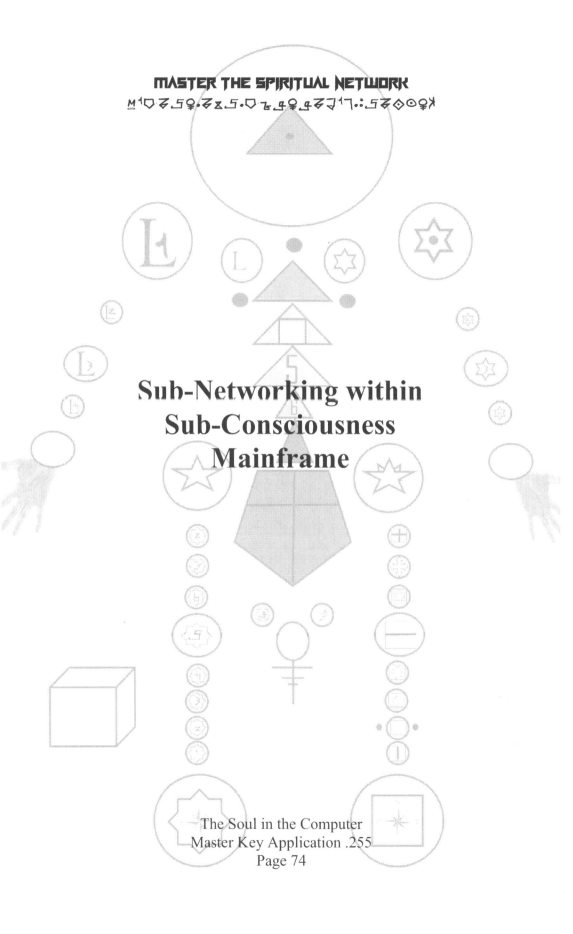

Sub-Networking within Sub-Consciousness Mainframe

: 1 Subnetting is the process of dividing a large network into smaller, more manageable pieces. Think of it like breaking up a large sandwich into smaller parts to share with others. Each subnet, like a piece of the sandwich, serves a specific purpose and can be distributed where needed. Spiritually, this is like breaking down the overwhelming aspects of life into manageable portions, where each aspect (or subnet) plays a role in a larger design. By understanding how to subnet, you can make your network, or your spiritual path, more organized and efficient.

Subnet Ma	CIDR Notat	Number of	Number of Subnets
255.0.0.0	/8	#########	1
255.128.0.	/9	8,388,606	2
255.192.0.	/10	4,194,302	4
255.224.0.	/11	2,097,150	8
255.240.0.	/12	1,048,574	16
255.248.0.	/13	524,286	32
255.252.0.	/14	262,142	64
255.254.0.	/15	131,070	128
255.255.0.	/16	65,534	256
255.255.12	/17	32,766	512
255.255.19	/18	16,382	1024
255.255.22	/19	8,190	2048
255.255.24	/20	4,094	4096
255.255.24	/21	2,046	8192
255.255.25	/22	1,022	16,384
255.255.25	/23	510	32,768
255.255.25	/24	254	65,536
255.255.25	/25	126	131,072
255.255.25	/26	62	262,144
255.255.25	/27	30	524,288
255.255.25	/28	14	1,048,576
255.255.25	/29	6	2,097,152
255.255.25	/30	2	4,194,304

:2 An IP subnet is a subset of a Class A, B, or C network. When subnetting, we take a large network, such as a Class B network (like 172.16.0.0), and divide it into smaller, more specific networks. Just as in life, where we divide our time into smaller segments for work, relationships, and self-reflection, subnetting organizes the network into smaller, dedicated spaces. This allows for better control and monitoring, ensuring that each "subnet" of our spiritual or technical life functions optimally.

:3 In the context of a large network, subnetting is used to divide resources. In a Class B network like 172.16.0.0, you might create subnets for different departments or functions, such as marketing, finance, or IT. These subnets allow each part of the organization to work independently, just like how different parts of our soul work together while maintaining their own purpose. Each subnet in a network allows specific tasks to be accomplished, akin to how each aspect of our spiritual journey leads us toward fulfillment.

:4 When planning subnets, it's essential to consider how many subnets and host addresses are required. This planning process is similar to understanding the various roles we play in life—each role requires its own "address" or identity. By assigning specific IP addresses to devices within each subnet, you're effectively giving each device a purpose, just as you assign purpose to the different parts of your life.

Subnet Ma	Wildcard M	CIDR Notation
255.0.0.0	0.255.255.	/8
255.128.0.	0.127.255.	/9
255.192.0.	0.63.255.2	/10
255.224.0.	0.31.255.2	/11
255.240.0.	0.15.255.2	/12
255.248.0.	0.7.255.25	/13
255.252.0.	0.3.255.25	/14
255.254.0.	0.1.255.25	/15
255.255.0.	0.0.255.25	/16
255.255.12	0.0.127.25	/17
255.255.19	0.0.63.255	/18
255.255.22	0.0.31.255	/19
255.255.24	0.0.15.255	/20
255.255.24	0.0.7.255	/21
255.255.25	0.0.3.255	/22
255.255.25	0.0.1.255	/23
255.255.25	0.0.0.255	/24
255.255.25	0.0.0.127	/25
255.255.25	0.0.0.63	/26
255.255.25	0.0.0.31	/27
255.255.25	0.0.0.15	/28
255.255.25	0.0.0.7	/29
255.255.25	0.0.0.3	/30

:5 In the operational view of subnetting, the key is to interpret the design decisions made earlier. For instance, understanding why certain subnets share the same first three octets helps you manage and operate the network better. Similarly, in life, reflecting on decisions made by higher powers or even ancestors allows you to navigate challenges with greater wisdom.

Understanding the structure helps us find meaning in both technical and spiritual contexts.

:6 Analyzing needs in subnetting involves asking critical questions: How many subnets are required? How many host addresses are needed? These questions are parallel to the spiritual queries we ask when organizing our lives—what are the key areas of focus, and what resources do we need to thrive? Planning the number of subnets is like planning our spiritual journeys, ensuring that each part of the network (or life) has enough resources to function properly.

:7 When grouping devices into subnets, it's essential to think of the purpose of each device or group. Devices that frequently communicate with one another should be in the same subnet, much like how like-minded people should share common goals. This helps with efficiency and reduces unnecessary traffic. Similarly, in our spiritual lives, grouping similar pursuits together brings clarity and allows for more direct communication with our higher purpose.

:8 The question of how many subnets an internetwork requires is similar to asking how many paths we need to fulfill our destiny. For each goal, there must be enough room for growth and development, just like each subnet needs a certain number of available IP addresses. Spirituality teaches us to be open to growth, and subnetting requires the same mindset—ensuring there's space for the unexpected.

:9 Just as there are rules about which devices should be grouped in a subnet, there are moral principles that dictate which aspects of life should be kept together. For example, work-life balance requires setting boundaries between professional and personal life, much like how subnetting requires logical divisions within a network. Keeping these boundaries allows for smoother functioning both in a network and in our lives.

:10 A network, like life, requires careful planning. When you design subnets, you take into account not only the present needs but also future growth. This mirrors the spiritual concept of planning ahead, considering both short-term goals and long-term destiny. Subnetting a network ensures that we do not run out of resources, just as preparing for the future ensures that we continue to grow spiritually.

:11 The process of subnetting mirrors the process of self-discovery. We take a large, undefined part of ourselves (a large network) and divide it into smaller, more defined aspects (subnets). This gives us the clarity to work on specific areas of life, just as subnets provide clarity in a network. Whether it's personal growth, relationships, or career, dividing and organizing helps us manage the complex journey of life.

:12 Planning the implementation of subnets includes assigning IP addresses, planning DHCP ranges, and setting subnet locations. In life, this is similar to setting boundaries, assigning responsibilities, and ensuring that everyone knows their role. When everything is in place, life (or a network) runs smoothly because everyone knows their purpose and the resources available to them.

:13 Just like in network design, the spiritual journey requires organization. Each subnet needs to have the right IP range, just as each area of our lives must be given the right amount of attention and energy. If we over-allocate or under-allocate, things become imbalanced. Similarly, balancing different aspects of life requires careful thought and planning to ensure harmony.

:14 In subnetting, we divide a large network into smaller parts to make it more manageable. Spiritually, this is like taking our chaotic lives and dividing them into manageable portions—work, family, health, spirituality—each with its own "address" or focus. By doing so, we ensure that every part of our lives is attended to, without becoming overwhelmed by the whole.

:15 When we set up subnets, we leave room for growth. This is crucial both in networks and in life. If we design subnets too tightly, there won't be enough room to expand. Similarly, if we live our lives without considering future growth, we limit our potential. Always leave room for expansion in your network, and in your spiritual life, leave room for personal and collective growth.

:16 Subnetting can be compared to moral discernment. Just as we need to decide which hosts go into which subnet, we must also decide which values, beliefs, and practices fit into different parts of our lives. Dividing them into subnets makes the overall system more manageable, much like compartmentalizing values helps us stay true to our core while navigating various paths.

:17 Planning IP subnetting requires careful analysis, just as planning life's journey requires deep introspection. Each subnet must be tailored to specific needs, just like how each part of our lives must be shaped according to our individual purpose. The clearer the design, the smoother the execution—both in networks and in the spiritual walk.

:18 Subnetting involves breaking down a network into smaller, more manageable pieces by using a **subnet mask**. The subnet mask tells the network which part of an IP address refers to the **network** and which part refers to the **host**. Each subnet mask has a different **prefix length**, such as **/23**, **/27**, or **/17**, which determines the number of bits used for the network and the number of bits available for hosts. Spiritually, this is like deciding how much of your energy is devoted to maintaining your foundation (network) versus the amount available to connect with others (hosts). By understanding the subnet mask, you can optimize both your technical and spiritual growth.

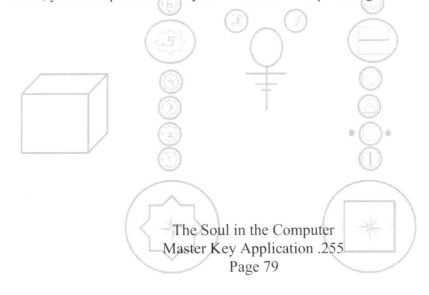

The Soul in the Computer
Master Key Application .255

:19 Let's start with **Class A, B, and C networks**. These represent different starting points for subnetting, just like how different individuals start their spiritual journeys from various life circumstances. Class A networks (such as 10.0.0.0/8) have a large number of host addresses available and are suitable for very large organizations. Class B (such as 172.16.0.0/16) and Class C (such as 192.168.1.0/24) networks have fewer host addresses but are more appropriate for smaller organizations or departments. This is like starting your spiritual journey with either a vast amount of resources (Class A) or a more focused, modest beginning (Class C), both of which have their own benefits and challenges.

:20 In a **Class A** network, only the first 8 bits are reserved for the **network portion**, leaving 24 bits for hosts. For example, a network like **10.0.0.0/8** can support up to **16,777,216** hosts. This is similar to having a vast spiritual capacity but needing careful management to avoid being overwhelmed. Just as a Class A network gives space for many hosts, in our lives, we need to balance the large spiritual opportunities we encounter with how we allocate our energy.

:21 A **Class B** network, such as **172.16.0.0/16**, reserves the first 16 bits for the network, leaving 16 bits for hosts. This means that a Class B network can support **65,536** hosts, making it ideal for medium-sized organizations. Spiritually, this is like having a well-balanced life where you can focus on both personal development and helping others without feeling overextended. You can manage a significant number of spiritual connections, but still, maintain a clear structure and purpose.

:22 A **Class C** network, like **192.168.1.0/24**, reserves the first 24 bits for the network, leaving only 8 bits for hosts. This supports up to **256** hosts and is more suitable for smaller networks. Spiritually, this is like focusing on a small, intimate group of relationships or practices. It's manageable and direct, allowing for deep connections without spreading yourself too thin. A Class C network is like building a small, sacred community where each person or practice is closely monitored and nurtured.

:23 Now, let's look at an example of subnetting using a /**23** subnet mask. A /**23** means that the first 23 bits are reserved for the network, and the remaining 9 bits are for hosts. This creates a network that can support up to **512** hosts ($2^9 = 512$). In a practical sense, this is like creating a spiritual practice where you are open to building a larger community, but you still maintain some control and structure. You have room for growth, but not so much that you become overwhelmed.

Example:

- IP Address: 192.168.0.0

- Subnet Mask: 255.255.254.0

- Network: 192.168.0.0/23

This subnetting allows for IP addresses ranging from 192.168.0.1 to 192.168.1.254. It is a large enough block to support two Class C networks combined but still small enough to manage.

:24 A **/27** subnet mask reserves the first 27 bits for the network, leaving 5 bits for hosts. This gives you up to **32** hosts ($2^5 = 32$). A **/27** network is perfect for a small group of devices, like a small department or section of a company. Spiritually, this is akin to creating a **sacred circle** or **small community** with clear boundaries and roles. There is a focused intention in a /27 subnet—each person or host has a specific purpose, and there is little room for waste or distraction.

Example:

- IP Address: 192.168.1.0

- Subnet Mask: 255.255.255.224

- Network: 192.168.1.0/27

This subnet allows for IP addresses ranging from 192.168.1.1 to 192.168.1.30, offering a tightly controlled environment with room for only a select group.

:25 A **/17** subnet mask reserves the first 17 bits for the network and leaves 15 bits for hosts. This gives a capacity of **32,768** hosts ($2^{15} = 32,768$). Spiritually, a **/17** subnet represents opening yourself up to a much larger mission or purpose. This subnet gives room for many connections, allowing for expansive growth and influence while maintaining a broad network of support.

Example:

- IP Address: 10.0.0.0

- Subnet Mask: 255.255.128.0

- Network: 10.0.0.0/17

This subnet allows for IP addresses from 10.0.0.1 to 10.0.127.254, creating a large and expansive network of devices and people who are interconnected yet grounded in a single, unified purpose.

:26 Each **block size** in subnetting refers to the number of available IP addresses within the subnet. For instance, a **/24** block gives you 256 addresses, a **/30** block gives you 4 addresses, and a **/16** block provides 65,536 addresses. These sizes represent how many connections you can manage or handle in your spiritual practice. Larger block sizes are suitable for expansive networks, while smaller blocks are ideal for more focused, intimate groups.

:27 When subnetting, it's important to balance the number of subnets with the number of available hosts. Too many subnets with too few hosts can lead to fragmentation, while too few subnets with many hosts can create inefficiency. Spiritually, this is like ensuring you don't spread yourself too thin across too many projects or people. It's about creating balance—knowing when to focus deeply and when to broaden your reach.

:28 Let's look at a real-world example using **Class B network 172.16.0.0/16**. If you subnet this network with a **/24** mask, you create subnets with **256 hosts** each. The first subnet would be **172.16.0.0/24**, the second would be **172.16.1.0/24**, and so on. This process allows for a large, medium-sized network to be divided into manageable pieces, each functioning like a small community. Spiritually, this represents dividing a large mission into specific, actionable steps, each with its own dedicated energy and focus.

:29 Similarly, if we took a **Class A network** like **10.0.0.0/8** and subnetted it with a **/17** mask, we would create subnets with **32,768 hosts** each. This is a much larger network, representing expansive growth and influence. Spiritually, this is like managing a larger organization or community, where many individuals come together under one shared vision.

:30 Subnetting gives you the power to design a network that fits your specific needs, just like spiritual practice allows you to design a life that fulfills your unique purpose. Each subnet represents a different aspect of your mission, with a clear path for expansion, security, and balance. Whether you are working with a small, intimate group or a vast network of people, understanding subnetting gives you the tools to connect and grow in a meaningful way.

SUBNETTING

:31 Understanding the **classes of IP addresses** and **block sizes** is essential for both networking and spiritual growth. **Class A networks** are like large, expansive missions; **Class B networks** are more balanced and manageable; and **Class C networks** are smaller, more intimate. By choosing the right subnet mask and dividing your network into subnets, you create a structure that allows for efficiency, growth, and balance—both in your technical life and your spiritual journey.

:32 When we look at **subnetting**, the idea of division is essential. In life, we often divide our focus into various aspects—personal growth, relationships, work, and spirituality. Each of these represents a different subnet within the larger network of our lives. In networking, subnetting is the process of dividing a larger network into smaller, manageable sub-networks, allowing for easier control and optimized traffic. Spiritually, this is akin to organizing our lives into balanced components, ensuring that each aspect functions without overwhelming the whole.

:33 **Subnetting** also helps manage traffic, similar to how mindfulness or discipline helps manage the flow of thoughts and energy in life. Without proper management, chaos ensues, whether in a network or your mental state. When you assign IP addresses to a subnet, you are designating that space for a specific purpose, just as you allocate time and attention to specific aspects of your life.

:34 Consider the **/24 subnet mask**, which provides 256 IP addresses, with 254 usable addresses. This can be likened to organizing a group of 254 individuals with specific roles and responsibilities, ensuring each has the resources they need to function. A **/24** subnet mask offers balance—enough space for medium-sized networks, much like how you balance various tasks throughout the day.

:35 In a more technical sense, subnetting helps create boundaries within a network. Using different subnet masks such as **/23** or **/27** allows you to determine how many devices can be part of that subnet. Think of this as drawing clear boundaries in relationships—knowing where your energy flows and where it stops, maintaining peace and balance.

:36 **Class A**, **Class B**, and **Class C** networks are like the stages of personal development. A **Class A** network, such as 10.0.0.0, is vast, like a person in the early stages of life with endless potential. **Class B** networks, such as 172.16.0.0, represent a more defined stage, where growth and responsibility increase. Finally, **Class C** networks, such as 192.168.0.0, signify a more focused and specialized point in life, where roles are clearer and paths more defined. Each class represents a phase in life, just as each subnet represents a distinct section within the network.

:37 **Subnet masks** define the size of a subnet, and their bit length (such as /24 or /27) determines how many devices can fit within that subnet. The smaller the subnet, the more focused it becomes. For example, a /30 subnet supports only 2 hosts, perfect for point-to-point communication between two devices. Spiritually, this can represent intimate, one-on-one connections, where focus is narrow but deep, such as close friendships or mentorships.

:38 On the other hand, a /16 subnet offers a much larger space, supporting up to 65,534 hosts. This would represent a larger, more diverse community, like a global movement or organization, where many individuals are connected by a common goal. Spiritually, this larger subnet reflects a broader sense of purpose or service, reaching beyond the personal to affect the collective.

:39 **Routing between subnets** is crucial in networking, just as maintaining healthy boundaries and communication between different aspects of your life is essential. A router helps move information between subnets, guiding traffic based on the destination address. In life, wisdom and clarity act as routers, directing energy and focus where it is needed most, ensuring that different areas of your life (like family and work) remain connected yet distinct.

:40 **Subnetting** is also about efficiency. Just as we strive to use our time wisely, a well-subnetted network avoids waste by using only the necessary IP addresses. A **/27** subnet, for example, provides 30 usable IP addresses—perfect for small teams or focused projects. This represents a spiritual principle of minimalism: use only what you need, keep things simple, and avoid excess.

:41 In networking, the **broadcast address** is the highest IP address in a subnet, used to communicate with all devices in that subnet. Think of the

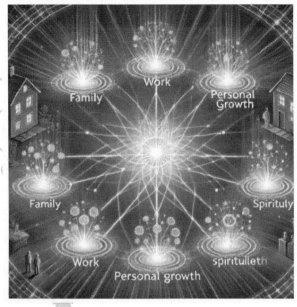

broadcast as your higher self or intuition sending a message to all parts of your being. The **network address** is the lowest address, representing the foundation—the starting point from which everything in that subnet emerges, much like your core values or spiritual grounding.

:42 Subnetting also prevents conflicts, just as setting boundaries in life prevents misunderstandings and miscommunication. By assigning different subnets, you ensure that devices (or aspects of your life) operate in harmony without stepping on each other's toes. This careful separation keeps networks, and personal energies, running smoothly.

:43 Now, let's look at how **subnetting** can apply in practice with specific examples. A **/23** subnet mask would give you 512 IP addresses with 510 usable addresses. This is ideal for medium-sized organizations, balancing growth potential with operational efficiency. It's like managing a medium-sized community where each person has their own role, yet the group remains connected through shared values or goals.

Example:

- IP Address: 172.16.0.0

- Subnet Mask: 255.255.254.0 (which corresponds to **/23**)

- Network Range: 172.16.0.1 to 172.16.1.254

:44 If we consider a **/17** subnet mask, we have even more space, allowing for 32,768 IP addresses. This type of subnet would be used in large organizations or for wide-reaching networks. Spiritually, this can represent a large-scale endeavor or purpose in life, where the reach is broad, and the potential for connection is immense.

> **Example**:

- IP Address: 192.168.0.0

- Subnet Mask: 255.255.128.0 (which corresponds to **/17**)

- Network Range: 192.168.0.

:44 In subnetting, we must assign IP addresses according to well-defined rules, just as we must live by certain principles to maintain balance in our lives. The first rule is that addresses in the same subnet are not separated by a router, meaning that they are part of the same network space. Spiritually, this is like individuals in close proximity sharing the same energy, able to communicate freely without barriers. But when two entities (or addresses) are in different subnets, a router—a boundary—is required to manage their communication.

:45 The router, then, becomes a symbol of discernment in life. It chooses which information or energy should pass between different parts of the network, much like how we decide what thoughts or emotions to share or withhold. Routing between subnets mirrors our ability to manage and navigate different roles or areas of our lives with wisdom and balance.

:46 Now, let's consider how subnets are created. To form subnets, we "borrow" bits from the host portion of the IP address, just like reallocating time or energy in life to focus on different priorities. In networking terms, borrowing host bits reduces the number of devices that can be in a subnet, but it increases the number of subnets, allowing for better organization and control.

:47 For example, in a **/24 subnet**, there are 256 possible addresses, but only 254 are usable for hosts because the first and last addresses are reserved. These reserved addresses represent the boundaries of the subnet—the **subnet ID** and **broadcast address**—which provide structure and prevent overlap, much like the boundaries we set in life to protect our personal space and energy.

:48 In a **/23 subnet**, we extend the range of usable addresses to 512, but again, two addresses are reserved. This larger subnet represents more potential connections, similar to expanding your social network or increasing the scale of a project. Spiritually, it reminds us that with greater capacity comes the need for even clearer boundaries and more careful management of resources.

:49 When working with subnet masks, we must choose wisely how many bits to allocate to the **network**, **subnet**, and **host** portions. This is like distributing your time and focus: you need to leave enough energy for yourself (hosts) while also maintaining relationships and responsibilities (subnets) within the greater context of your life (the network). The balance you choose will determine how effectively you can manage all parts of your existence.

:50 Let's dive into the practical example of a /23 subnet. With 512 total addresses and 510 usable, this is perfect for a medium-sized organization, where the network needs to grow and support more devices. Spiritually, this can be likened to managing a large community or network of people, where everyone has a place, but the connections must be carefully organized to avoid chaos.

Example:

- IP Address: 172.16.0.0

- Subnet Mask: 255.255.254.0 (or **/23**)

- Usable Addresses: 172.16.0.1 to 172.16.1.254

:51 In this **/23** subnet example, the **subnet ID** (172.16.0.0) marks the boundary of this smaller world within the larger network. Just like defining goals and purposes in life, the subnet ID clarifies the starting point of a focused endeavor. The **broadcast address** (172.16.1.255) ensures that communication reaches every device in the subnet, much like how your energy radiates to those around you when you're fully present and focused.

:52 Similarly, in a **/17 subnet**, we see a larger scale, with over 32,000 usable addresses. This subnet represents an expansive network, like managing a larger enterprise or community, where organization is key. Spiritually, a **/17** subnet mirrors the broader reach of a person who has influence over many, but still requires clear structure to ensure that everything operates smoothly.

Example:

- IP Address: 192.168.0.0

- Subnet Mask: 255.255.128.0 (or **/17**)

- Usable Addresses: 192.168.0.1 to 192.168.127.254

:53 When we borrow **host bits** to create more subnets, we are making a trade-off between the number of devices we can support and the number of distinct networks we can manage. This is akin to dividing your attention between different aspects of life—choosing whether to focus on fewer things with greater depth or to broaden your scope and manage more areas simultaneously.

:54 Take, for example, a **/27 subnet**. This subnet supports only 30 usable addresses, which is ideal for small, focused projects or teams. Spiritually, a **/27** subnet could represent a close-knit group, where each person has a unique role, and communication flows easily because the group is small enough for everyone to be in sync.

Example:

- IP Address: 192.168.1.0

- Subnet Mask: 255.255.255.224 (or **/27**)

- Usable Addresses: 192.168.1.1 to 192.168.1.30

:55 Subnets, much like different aspects of our lives, need to be properly maintained and secured. Without boundaries or proper management, communication breaks down, and conflicts arise. In a network, **routers** provide the boundaries that keep subnets isolated but still connected through controlled paths. In life, our personal values and principles act as routers, ensuring that our interactions with others are positive and that we maintain our integrity while navigating the complexities of the world.

:56 Subnetting is more than just a technical exercise; it's a way of organizing life. Just as you break down a network into subnets for easier management, you must also break down the components of your life into manageable pieces, ensuring each has enough attention and resources to thrive. By setting proper boundaries and maintaining clear connections, both networks and lives run smoothly, with each subnet (or aspect) operating in harmony with the whole.

:57 In life, the concept of subnetting mirrors how we must allocate our energy and focus. Just as we assign IP addresses to specific subnets to organize and direct communication within a network, we must also assign our attention to the different aspects of our lives. Each subnet, like each area of life, requires a certain level of attention and resources. Whether it's work, family, or personal growth, it's important to define clear boundaries and ensure that each part receives what it needs to function efficiently.

:58 A **Class A network**, for example, provides a large number of IP addresses (over 16 million) and is typically used in very large organizations. Spiritually, this could represent a person or entity with vast influence and resources, able to manage many different aspects or subnets. However, with great capacity comes the need for even greater discernment in how those resources are divided and managed.

Example:

- Class A IP Address: 10.0.0.0

- Subnet Mask: 255.0.0.0 (or **/8**)

- Usable Addresses: 10.0.0.1 to 10.255.255.254

:59 A **Class B network** is more moderate, supporting up to 65,534 addresses. This network type might represent a person with a well-balanced life, managing multiple roles and responsibilities but within a more contained environment. The spiritual equivalent here could be someone who balances family, career, and personal pursuits, ensuring that each area is attended to without overwhelming the system.

Example:

- Class B IP Address: 172.16.0.0

- Subnet Mask: 255.255.0.0 (or **/16**)

- Usable Addresses: 172.16.0.1 to 172.16.255.254

:60 A **Class C network**, with its smaller block of addresses (up to 254 usable), might represent a more focused individual or team, working on specialized tasks or projects. There's less need for broad influence, but more attention to detail within a specific domain. This could be likened to an artist or craftsman who focuses deeply on their craft, ensuring that every element within their smaller "subnet" is perfectly aligned.

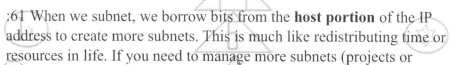

Example:

- Class C IP Address: 192.168.1.0

- Subnet Mask: 255.255.255.0 (or **/24**)

- Usable Addresses: 192.168.1.1 to 192.168.1.254

:61 When we subnet, we borrow bits from the **host portion** of the IP address to create more subnets. This is much like redistributing time or resources in life. If you need to manage more subnets (projects or relationships), you may have to take some resources away from other areas. The key is balance: ensuring that each subnet (aspect of life) has enough to thrive without overburdening the network (your energy and attention).

:62 For example, in a **/24 subnet**, there are 254 usable addresses. If you borrow 2 bits for subnetting, you can create 4 subnets, each with 62 usable addresses. In life, this is like taking a large goal and breaking it into 4 smaller, more manageable parts. Each part still has its own capacity for growth, but you have divided your resources in a way that makes the goal achievable.

Example:

- Subnet Mask: 255.255.255.192 (or **/26**)
- Usable Addresses Per Subnet: 62

:63 Borrowing more bits creates smaller subnets with fewer addresses, which is ideal for focused tasks or small teams. For example, in a **/28 subnet**, you only have 14 usable addresses, but you can create many more subnets. This is similar to focusing deeply on one or two small tasks at a time, rather than spreading yourself too thin across many large projects.

Example:

- Subnet Mask: 255.255.255.240 (or **/28**)
- Usable Addresses Per Subnet: 14

:64 Spiritually, subnetting can be seen as the practice of mindfulness—breaking down the vastness of life into smaller, more digestible pieces that we can focus on one at a time. By setting clear boundaries, we prevent overwhelm and ensure that each part of our network (life) functions properly, with clear communication between all parts.

:65 The process of assigning subnet masks is like setting intentions or goals. Just as a subnet mask defines the size and capacity of a subnet, our intentions define the scope of what we aim to achieve. If the mask is too large, resources may be wasted; if it's too small, the subnet might become overcrowded and inefficient. The key is to assign the right amount of focus and energy to each area.

:66 The **subnet broadcast address** is the address used to send a message to all devices in the subnet. Spiritually, this represents the act of sharing wisdom or guidance with a larger group. Just as a broadcast address ensures that every device in the subnet receives the same message, sharing spiritual insights can help uplift and guide others within your community or network.

:67 Subnetting also teaches us about **boundaries**. Just as each subnet has clear limits defined by its subnet mask, we too must define the boundaries of our time, energy, and focus. Without proper boundaries, our resources become diluted, and our ability to function efficiently is compromised. By subnetting our lives—allocating time and attention to specific areas—we can ensure that each part is nurtured and supported.

:68 In the same way that routers direct traffic between subnets, our principles and values direct our actions and decisions. The **router** becomes a symbol of wisdom, discerning which connections and communications should be allowed and which should be blocked. It ensures that the various parts of our lives remain connected in a healthy and organized manner.

:69 **Subnetting** is not just a technical practice but a spiritual one as well. It teaches us to organize, prioritize, and manage our lives in a way that allows for growth, connection, and harmony. Just as we assign IP addresses and masks to manage network traffic, we must assign time, energy, and focus to the different aspects of our lives, ensuring that everything runs smoothly and with purpose.

:70 Subnetting is a foundational aspect of IP networking, breaking a larger network into smaller, more manageable subnets. At its core, subnetting is about efficient use of resources. In an IP network, addresses are a finite resource, and subnetting ensures that they are allocated appropriately, allowing a network to scale effectively. This division also provides structure, security, and control over how data is routed within and between different segments of the network.

:71 A **subnet mask** determines how many bits of an IP address are used for the network portion and how many are used for the host portion. In a subnet, the network portion is the same for all devices, while the host portion is unique to each device. The subnet mask helps devices determine whether the IP address they are trying to communicate with is on the same network or if the communication needs to be routed through a gateway.

:72 Subnetting allows for the creation of multiple smaller networks within a larger network, which has many practical applications. In a corporate environment, for example, different departments might need to be on separate subnets to isolate their traffic, improve performance, or implement security policies. Each subnet acts as a distinct entity, even though it is part of the same overarching network.

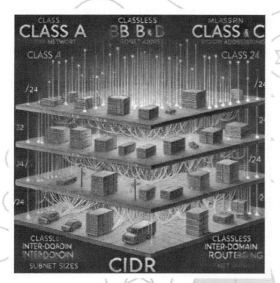

:73 The **Class A, B, and C networks** represent different network sizes, with Class A being the largest and Class C being the smallest. The choice of which class to use depends on the size of the network and how many devices it needs to support. In modern networking, classful addressing has largely been replaced by **Classless Inter-Domain Routing (CIDR)**, which allows for more flexible subnetting by not adhering to the strict class boundaries.

:74 **CIDR** uses the notation **/x**, where "x" represents the number of bits in the network portion of the IP address. For example, **/24** means the first 24 bits of the IP address are reserved for the network, and the remaining bits are for hosts. This system provides more granular control over how IP addresses are allocated and is essential in managing today's networks, which need to support varying sizes of subnets.

:75 When subnetting, the main goal is to balance the number of **subnets** and the number of **hosts** per subnet. The more bits you borrow from the host portion to create subnets, the fewer hosts you can have in each subnet. Conversely, the fewer bits you borrow, the more hosts each subnet can accommodate. This trade-off must be carefully considered based on the specific needs of the network.

:76 For example, using a **/27** subnet mask means that 27 bits are allocated for the network and subnet portion, leaving 5 bits for the host portion.

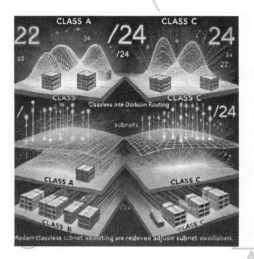

This gives you 32 possible IP addresses, but only 30 can be used for devices, as two addresses are reserved: one for the subnet ID and one for the broadcast address. A **/23** subnet mask, on the other hand, leaves 9 bits for the host portion, allowing for 510 usable IP addresses in each subnet.

Example:

- **/27 Subnet**: 255.255.255.224 (30 usable IP addresses)

- **/23 Subnet**: 255.255.254.0 (510 usable IP addresses)

:77 Subnetting also provides more control over **network traffic**. Devices within the same subnet can communicate directly with each other without needing to go through a router. However, if a device on one subnet wants to communicate with a device on another subnet, that traffic must pass through a router. This structure allows network administrators to control which devices can communicate directly and which must go through additional layers of security or monitoring.

:78 **Subnetting's role in security** is essential, especially in large networks. By dividing a network into subnets, you can isolate sensitive data, limit the spread of security breaches, and reduce the scope of potential attacks. For example, critical infrastructure such as servers can be placed on a separate subnet from user devices, ensuring that only authorized traffic reaches them.

:79 **Route summarization** is another benefit of subnetting. In larger networks, routing tables can become very large, making the process of finding the correct route slower and more complex. Subnetting allows for **aggregation of routes**. For instance, a group of subnets can be summarized as a single entry in a routing table, reducing the size of the table and improving the efficiency of routing. This is particularly useful in large, geographically distributed networks.

:80 When subnetting, it's important to understand how **subnet masks** impact routing. A subnet mask defines how many bits of an IP address are used for identifying the network and how many are used for identifying the hosts within that network. For example, a **/24** subnet mask means that the first 24 bits are reserved for the network portion, leaving 8 bits for the host portion. This results in 256 total IP addresses, of which 254 can be assigned to devices.

.81 Subnetting enables network administrators to **segment network traffic**, improve performance, and enhance security. It's not just about dividing networks but also about designing the flow of communication in a way that optimizes resources. In an enterprise network, subnetting can help ensure that high-priority traffic, such as data from critical applications, is not slowed down by less important traffic.

:82 The **broadcast address** in each subnet is used to send messages to all devices in that subnet. This concept is particularly important in **local area networks (LANs)**, where broadcasting is used for functions such as **address resolution protocol (ARP)**, which maps IP addresses to MAC addresses. While useful, excessive broadcasting can slow down the network, which is why subnetting can be used to limit the size of broadcast domains.

:83 Subnetting and **address planning** go hand in hand. Before deploying a network, administrators need to plan how many subnets they will need, how many hosts each subnet will support, and how the IP address space will be allocated. This planning ensures that the network can scale as the organization grows and that IP addresses are used efficiently.

:84 **VLANs (Virtual Local Area Networks)** often work in tandem with subnetting. VLANs allow administrators to segment a physical network into multiple logical networks. Devices on the same VLAN can communicate as if they were on the same physical network, even if they are spread across different locations. Each VLAN typically has its own subnet, further enhancing the control and management of network traffic.

:85 The ability to **expand or contract** subnets is also an important feature of subnetting. As network requirements change, subnets can be adjusted to accommodate more or fewer hosts. For instance, if a department grows, its subnet can be expanded by changing the subnet mask to allocate more IP addresses. This flexibility ensures that the network can adapt to organizational needs without requiring a complete redesign.

:86 Finally, understanding **subnetting is essential** for achieving network efficiency. It allows you to allocate the right amount of IP addresses to the right places, ensuring that the network can grow while minimizing waste. Whether in a small business network or a large enterprise, subnetting provides the structure needed to ensure smooth and secure communication across all devices.

:87 The subnet mask divides the IP address into network and host portions. In classful addressing, the mask defines how many bits belong to the network and how many are left for hosts. However, when subnetting, we borrow bits from the host portion to create more subnets. This is crucial when you need to organize a network into smaller segments.

:88 In Class A, the first octet (8 bits) is reserved for the network, leaving 24 bits for hosts. A Class B address has the first 16 bits for the network, and 16 bits for hosts. Class C has the first 24 bits for the network and only 8 bits for hosts. Subnetting alters this, taking bits from the host portion to create subnets.

:89 Let's walk through a more detailed example using different subnet masks and classes. First, consider a Class A network. A Class A IP address might be 10.0.0.0, and its default subnet mask is 255.0.0.0, which leaves 24 bits for host addressing. If you borrow 8 bits for subnetting, the new subnet mask would be 255.255.0.0 (/16). This creates 2^8 or 256 subnets, each with $2^{16} - 2$ usable host addresses (65,534 hosts per subnet).

:90 Consider the same concept with Class B. A Class B network such as 172.16.0.0 has a default subnet mask of 255.255.0.0. If you borrow 4 bits from the host portion, the new subnet mask becomes 255.255.240.0 (/20). This results in 2^4 or 16 subnets, with $2^{12} - 2$ usable hosts per subnet (4094 hosts per subnet).

:91 Now let's move to a Class C address, where the network portion is already 24 bits. A Class C address like 192.168.1.0 has a default subnet mask of 255.255.255.0. Borrowing 3 bits from the host portion gives you a subnet mask of 255.255.255.224 (/27). This creates 2^3 or 8 subnets, each with $2^5 - 2$ usable hosts (30 hosts per subnet).

Subnetting Examples with Different Masks

:92 **Class A Example (Mask: /18, Subnet Mask: 255.255.192.0)**
Borrowing 10 bits from the host portion of a Class A address:

- Network: 10.0.0.0

- New Subnet Mask: 255.255.192.0 (/18)

- Number of subnets: $2^{10} = 1024$

- Hosts per subnet: $2^{14} - 2 = 16,382$ hosts

:93 **Class B Example (Mask: /21, Subnet Mask: 255.255.248.0)**
Borrowing 5 bits from the host portion of a Class B address:

- Network: 172.16.0.0

- New Subnet Mask: 255.255.248.0 (/21)

- Number of subnets: $2^5 = 32$

- Hosts per subnet: $2^{11} - 2 = 2046$ hosts

:94 Class C Example (Mask: /26, Subnet Mask: 255.255.255.192)

Borrowing 2 bits from the host portion of a Class C address:

- Network: 192.168.1.0

- New Subnet Mask: 255.255.255.192 (/26)

- Number of subnets: $2^2 = 4$

- Hosts per subnet: $2^6 - 2 = 62$ hosts

Subnetting Basics Recap:

When you create subnets, you divide a network into smaller, more manageable parts. The subnet mask tells us how many

Command Examples for Configuring Subnets

:95 Example 1: Creating VLANs on a Switch (VLAN 10, VLAN 20, VLAN 30)

Switch(config)# vlan 10

Switch(config-vlan)# name Messiah

Switch(config)# vlan 20

Switch(config-vlan)# name Peace

Switch(config)# vlan 30

Switch(config-vlan)# name Love

:97 Example 3: Configuring DHCP Pool for Subnet

```
Router(config)# ip dhcp pool body
Router(dhcp-config)# network 192.168.1.0 255.255.255.0
Router(dhcp-config)# default-router 192.168.1.1
Router(dhcp-config)# dns-server 8.8.8.8
```

:98 **Example 4: Creating a Static Route**

```
Router(config)# ip route 10.0.0.0 255.255.255.0 192.168.1.2
```

:99 **Example 5: Configuring Access Control Lists (ACLs)**

```
Router(config)# access-list 100 permit ip 192.168.1.0 0.0.0.255 any
Router(config)# access-list 100 deny ip 192.168.2.0 0.0.0.255 any
```

:100 **Example 6: Configuring OSPF Routing Protocol**

```
Router(config)# router ospf 1
Router(config-router)# network 192.168.1.0 0.0.0.255 area 0
Router(config-router)# network 10.0.0.0 0.255.255.255 area 0
```

:101 **Example 7: Assigning Static IPs to Host PCs**

```
PC(config)# ip address 172.16.1.10 255.255.255.0
PC(config)# default-gateway 172.16.1.1
```

:102 **Example 8: Configuring SSH on a Switch**

```
Switch(config)# ip domain-name example.com
Switch(config)# crypto key generate rsa
Switch(config)# username admin secret password123
Switch(config)# line vty 0 15
Switch(config-line)# login local
```

Switch(config-line)# transport input ssh

:103 **Example 9: Setting Up EtherChannel**

Switch(config)# interface range fa0/1 - 2

Switch(config-if-range)# channel-group 1 mode active

Switch(config-if-range)# exit

Switch(config)# interface port-channel 1

Switch(config-if)# switchport mode trunk

:104 **Example 10: Setting Up a Subnet on Router for a Small Network**

Router(config)# interface gig0/0

Router(config-if)# ip address 172.16.5.1 255.255.255.248

Router(config-if)# no shutdown

:105 **Example 11: Configure Loopback Interface for Testing**

Router(config)# interface loopback0

Router(config-if)# ip address 192.168.100.1 255.255.255.255

:106 **Example 12: Configuring VTP on Switch for VLAN Management**

Switch(config)# vtp domain MESSIAH_DOMAIN

Switch(config)# vtp mode server

:107 **Example 13: Setting Up HSRP (Hot Standby Router Protocol)**

Router(config)# interface gig0/0

Router(config-if)# standby 1 ip 10.1.1.254

Router(config-if)# standby 1 priority 110

Router(config-if)# standby 1 preempt

The Soul in the Computer
Master Key Application .255
Page 106

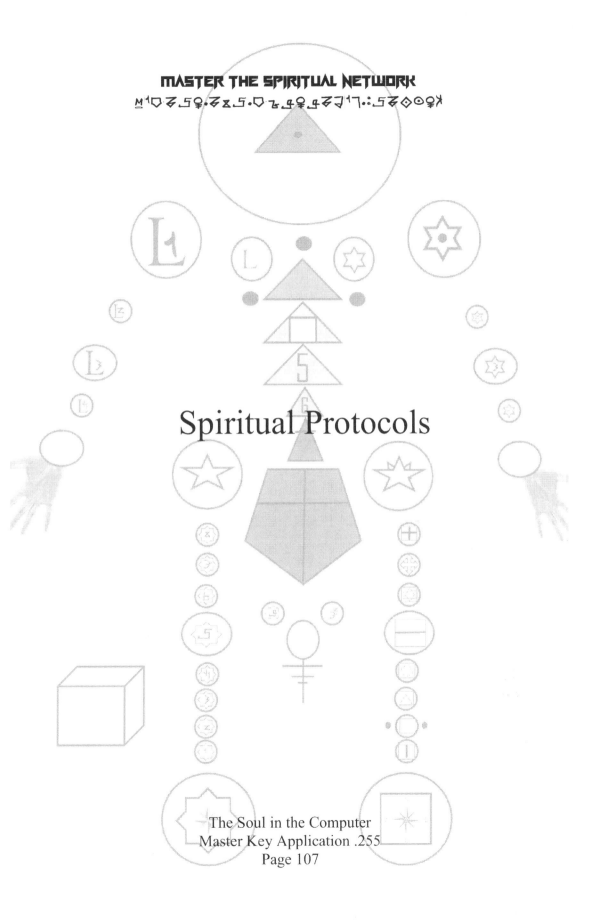

Spiritual Protocols

:1 TCP (Transmission Control Protocol)

Purpose: Ensures reliable communication by establishing a connection before data is transmitted, guaranteeing all packets are delivered in the correct order.

Spiritual Proverb: "A strong foundation is laid before a house is built; trust binds every stone to its rightful place."

:2 UDP (User Datagram Protocol)

Purpose: A connectionless protocol that sends data without ensuring delivery, prioritizing speed over reliability.

Spiritual Proverb: "The wind carries the message swiftly, not knowing if it will reach its destined ear, but trusting in the journey."

:3 DNS (Domain Name System)

Purpose: Translates human-friendly domain names into IP addresses so that devices can communicate on the network.

Spiritual Proverb: "In the search for meaning, names are but signposts to the deeper truths that guide us home."

:4 ARP (Address Resolution Protocol)

Purpose: Resolves an IP address to a physical MAC address, allowing devices on the same network to communicate.

Spiritual Proverb: "Every soul wears a mask, but beyond appearances lies the true essence known to those who seek."

:5 ICMP (Internet Control Message Protocol)

Purpose: Used for error reporting and diagnostics, ensuring devices can communicate any issues or failures in data transmission.

Spiritual Proverb: "The wise traveler listens for the warnings of the wind, for in the echo of silence, danger may lie."

:6 HTTP (Hypertext Transfer Protocol)

Purpose: Facilitates the transfer of data over the web, enabling users to access websites and content.

ᴍ¹◇⟋⌇◑·⟋⫿⌇·◇ ⟍·◮◑·⫿⟋⫿⟋◌¹◌¨·⌇⟋◇◇◑◉⟓

Spiritual Proverb: "The door to knowledge opens to those who seek, and every path taken leads to a greater understanding."

:7 HTTPS (Hypertext Transfer Protocol Secure)

Purpose: A secure version of HTTP that encrypts communication, ensuring data integrity and privacy.

Spiritual Proverb: "Guard your heart and your words, for what is spoken in trust should be shielded from the unworthy."

:8 SSH (Secure Shell)

Purpose: Provides secure, encrypted remote access to devices on a network, ensuring privacy and integrity during communication.

Spiritual Proverb: "True wisdom speaks in whispers, heard only by those who walk the path of trust and vigilance."

:9 FTP (File Transfer Protocol)

Purpose: Allows the transfer of files between a client and a server over a network, often requiring authentication.

Spiritual Proverb: "What is shared between hands must be trusted, for in the exchange of knowledge, hearts are enriched."

:10 TFTP (Trivial File Transfer Protocol)

Purpose: A simpler, faster file transfer protocol often used for transferring boot files or configurations between devices.

Spiritual Proverb: "Even the lightest load, carried with purpose, brings nourishment to those in need."

:11 DHCP (Dynamic Host Configuration Protocol)

Purpose: Automatically assigns IP addresses to devices on a network, ensuring efficient network management.

Spiritual Proverb: "In the flow of abundance, each one is given what they need to flourish in their rightful place."

:12 NTP (Network Time Protocol)

Purpose: Synchronizes the clocks of devices on a network, ensuring accurate timekeeping across systems.

Spiritual Proverb: "When all follow the rhythm of time, harmony prevails, and every step leads to unity."

:13 BGP (Border Gateway Protocol)

Purpose: Manages how packets are routed across the internet by exchanging routing information between different networks.
Spiritual Proverb: "The traveler knows many roads, but walks with wisdom, guiding others to the heart of their journey."

:14 EIGRP (Enhanced Interior Gateway Routing Protocol)

Purpose: A Cisco protocol used for dynamic routing, offering fast convergence and reduced bandwidth usage.
Spiritual Proverb: "The fastest path is not always the loudest, for quiet wisdom seeks the shortest way home."

:15 OSPF (Open Shortest Path First)

Purpose: A link-state routing protocol that finds the most efficient path for data within a network.
Spiritual Proverb: "A wise guide always seeks the clearest path, for clarity brings swift passage to the destination."

:16 RIP (Routing Information Protocol)

Purpose: A distance-vector routing protocol that sends routing information based on hop count.
Spiritual Proverb: "Step by step, the journey unfolds; though the way may be long, each step brings you closer to home."

:17 SNMP (Simple Network Management Protocol)

Purpose: Monitors and manages devices on a network by collecting and organizing information about them.
Spiritual Proverb: "To oversee the flock, the shepherd must know every lamb, for in knowing the whole, peace is maintained."

:18 SMTP (Simple Mail Transfer Protocol)

Purpose: Used to send and relay emails across networks.

ᴹ⁴♡ᵶ⌇♀∙ᵶᵶ⌇♡ᵶᵶ♀ᵶᵶ⌐⁴ᵔ∴⌇ᵶ◇◍♀⅄

Spiritual Proverb: "Words sent forth with purpose find their way, and even the smallest message may bring great meaning."

:19 IMAP (Internet Message Access Protocol)

Purpose: Allows users to access and manage their email messages stored on a remote server.

Spiritual Proverb: "What is stored with care may be retrieved when needed, for knowledge waits patiently to serve the seeker."

:20 POP3 (Post Office Protocol 3)

Purpose: Downloads emails from a server to a local device, often removing the email from the server afterward.

Spiritual Proverb: "What is received with gratitude must be held close, for once shared, the moment may pass, but the wisdom remains."

:21 SIP (Session Initiation Protocol)

Purpose: Initiates and manages multimedia communication sessions such as voice and video calls.

Spiritual Proverb: "Connections begin with a call, and in each meeting, there is the potential for growth and deeper understanding."

:22 RDP (Remote Desktop Protocol)

Purpose: Enables remote access and control of another computer's desktop over a network.

Spiritual Proverb: "Though distance separates, the spirit connects, allowing one to touch and guide from afar."

:23 IGMP (Internet Group Management Protocol)

Purpose: Manages the membership of hosts and routers in multicast groups, facilitating efficient data transmission to multiple destinations.

Spiritual Proverb: "When the many gather to listen, the message spreads far and wide, carried on the winds of unity."

:24 LLDP (Link Layer Discovery Protocol)

Purpose: Helps network devices discover each other and exchange basic information, often used to map network topology.

The Soul in the Computer
Master Key Application .255

Spiritual Proverb: "In knowing your neighbor, you find your place in the grand design, where connection leads to shared purpose."

:25 CDP (Cisco Discovery Protocol)
Purpose: A Cisco-proprietary protocol that allows devices to share information about directly connected devices.
Spiritual Proverb: "True power comes not from isolation, but from the knowledge of those who stand beside you."

:26 VRRP (Virtual Router Redundancy Protocol)
Purpose: Increases network reliability by creating virtual routers that act as backups for real routers in case of failure.
Spiritual Proverb: "When one falters, another rises, for strength lies in the shared commitment to continuity."

:27 HSRP (Hot Standby Router Protocol)
Purpose: A Cisco protocol that provides network redundancy by ensuring that a backup router is available in case the primary router fails.
Spiritual Proverb: "The wise leader prepares a successor, ensuring the path remains clear, even in moments of transition."

:28 FHRP (First Hop Redundancy Protocol)
Purpose: A family of protocols (including VRRP and HSRP) that ensures continuous availability of the default gateway for hosts.
Spiritual Proverb: "Though paths may diverge, the journey remains steady when there is always a guide to lead the way."

:29 MPLS (Multiprotocol Label Switching)
Purpose: Directs data between nodes in a network using short path labels instead of long network addresses, improving speed and efficiency.
Spiritual Proverb: "A clear path leads to swift passage, where burdens are lightened by the knowledge of where to go next."

:30 QoS (Quality of Service)
Purpose: Manages bandwidth and prioritizes critical network traffic, ensuring important data is transmitted with priority.

Spiritual Proverb: "In the balance of life, the important must rise above the trivial, for harmony is found in giving what is needed its due weight."

:31 NAT (Network Address Translation)

Purpose: Translates private IP addresses to a public IP address, allowing multiple devices on a private network to share a single public IP.
Spiritual Proverb: "In the heart of transformation, the many become one, crossing the boundaries of worlds unseen yet connected."

:32 PAT (Port Address Translation)

Purpose: A type of NAT that maps multiple private IP addresses to a single public IP address by using different ports.
Spiritual Proverb: "Many voices speak through a single gate, each carrying its message with clarity, though they pass through the same door."

:33 VTP (VLAN Trunking Protocol)

Purpose: Manages VLAN information across switches, ensuring consistent configuration throughout a network.
Spiritual Proverb: "When unity is maintained, all branches thrive, for in the shared foundation lies the strength of the whole."

:34 STP (Spanning Tree Protocol)

Purpose: Prevents network loops by creating a loop-free logical topology for Ethernet networks.
Spiritual Proverb: "The tree stands tall because its roots are grounded, avoiding the confusion of tangled branches."

:35 RSTP (Rapid Spanning Tree Protocol)

Purpose: An enhanced version of STP that reduces the time it takes to restore a loop-free network topology after changes.
Spiritual Proverb: "Quick to act, the wise prevent chaos before it spreads, restoring balance in the blink of an eye."

:36 VLAN (Virtual Local Area Network)

Purpose: Segments a physical network into logical networks to improve performance and security.

Spiritual Proverb: "Though we walk the same path, our purposes may differ; separation brings focus, and in focus, strength."

:37 PPP (Point-to-Point Protocol)

Purpose: Provides a standard method for transporting network layer data over point-to-point links.

Spiritual Proverb: "The bridge between two hearts is made stronger by understanding, where each step taken is guided by trust."

:38 GRE (Generic Routing Encapsulation)

Purpose: Encapsulates various network layer protocols to create point-to-point connections over an IP network.

Spiritual Proverb: "The path unseen connects the distant, veiled in simplicity but rich in purpose, carrying all who seek passage."

:39 LACP (Link Aggregation Control Protocol)

Purpose: Combines multiple physical links into a single logical link to increase bandwidth and provide redundancy.

Spiritual Proverb: "The strength of the chain lies not in one link, but in the many, for together they bear the weight of the journey."

:40 IGRP (Interior Gateway Routing Protocol)

Purpose: A Cisco protocol used for exchanging routing information within an autonomous system.

Spiritual Proverb: "The guide knows the paths within his own land, and with every turn, he leads his people with certainty and care."

The Soul in the Computer
Master Key Application .255

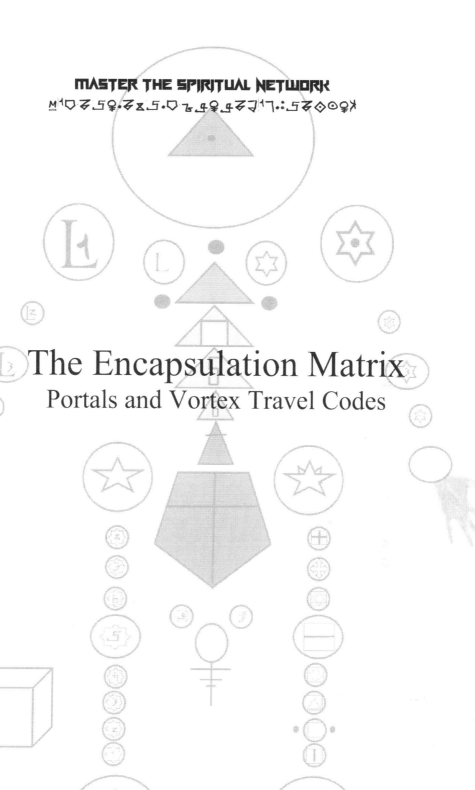

The Encapsulation Matrix
Portals and Vortex Travel Codes

:1 The Seven Layers of the OSI Model

Before diving into the encapsulation process, let's first list the seven layers of the OSI model, which describe how data travels from one device to another in a network:

Physical Layer (Layer 1): Responsible for transmitting raw bitstreams over a physical medium (**like cables or radio waves**).

Data Link Layer (Layer 2): Handles node-to-node data transfer and error detection, through mechanisms like MAC addresses.

Network Layer (Layer 3): Manages routing, addressing, and packet forwarding using logical addressing (**IP addresses**).

Transport Layer (Layer 4): Ensures reliable transmission of data between hosts, using protocols like **TCP** and **UDP**.

Session Layer (Layer 5): Manages sessions or connections between applications.

Presentation Layer (Layer 6): Translates, encrypts, and formats data for the application layer.

Application Layer (Layer 7): Provides network services directly to end users (e.g., HTTP, FTP, SMTP).

Encapsulation Process

:2 Step 1: Data at the Application Layer (Layer 7)

The encapsulation process begins at the application layer, where the data is generated by applications like web browsers, email clients, or file transfer programs. At this stage, the data is in its raw form, as the message or content you wish to send (e.g., an email or a web page).

Spiritual Analogy: "In the beginning, all things are pure intentions. The message starts as a simple thought or expression, unburdened by the complexities of delivery."

:3 Step 2: Presentation and Session Layers (Layers 6 and 5)

The presentation layer takes the raw data and prepares it for transmission by translating, compressing, or encrypting it. The session layer establishes and maintains communication between devices, ensuring that the data flow remains uninterrupted.

Spiritual Analogy: "Before we speak, our intentions are shaped by wisdom and understanding, creating a channel through which we can be heard clearly and securely."

:4 Step 3: Segmenting at the Transport Layer (Layer 4)

At the transport layer, the raw data is broken into smaller segments (if using TCP) or datagrams (if using UDP). TCP segments include mechanisms for ensuring reliable delivery, such as error checking and acknowledgments, while UDP is faster but does not guarantee delivery. The source and destination port numbers are also added to ensure that the data reaches the correct application on the receiving end.

Spiritual Analogy: "Just as a wise teacher breaks down complex ideas into understandable parts, the data is divided into segments so that it can be easily processed by the receiver."

:5 Step 4: Packaging into Packets at the Network Layer (Layer 3)

Once the data is segmented, the network layer encapsulates each segment into a packet, adding the source and destination IP addresses. This is where routing decisions are made, as the packet now contains the information it needs to navigate the network and find its destination.

Spiritual Analogy: "With direction and purpose, the traveler sets out on their journey, guided by the stars. So too does the data follow a path set by its destination."

:6 Step 5: Framing at the Data Link Layer (Layer 2)

At the data link layer, the packets are encapsulated into frames, which include source and destination MAC addresses. The frame is responsible for moving the data from one node to another within the same network or across connected networks.

Spiritual Analogy: "Before we can reach the distant horizon, we must pass through the gates of our immediate surroundings, carried by the strength of our local connections."

:7 Step 6: Transmission at the Physical Layer (Layer 1)

Finally, the frame is converted into bits—electrical signals, light pulses, or radio waves—depending on the medium being used. These bits are transmitted across the physical medium (e.g., copper cables, fiber optics, or airwaves), carrying the data to its next destination.

Spiritual Analogy: "Like the wind carrying seeds across the land, the physical transmission of data moves invisibly, yet with purpose, connecting distant lands."

Decapsulation: The Return Journey

:8 Step 7: Decapsulation at the Destination

Once the data reaches its destination, the process is reversed, with each layer removing its respective header or trailer, eventually delivering the raw data back to the application layer at the receiving end.

Spiritual Analogy: "As a wise receiver unravels the layers of experience to find the core truth, the destination removes each layer of encapsulation, revealing the message within."

Key Elements of Encapsulation

:9 Transport Layer Protocols: TCP vs. UDP

- **TCP (Transmission Control Protocol):** TCP is a connection-oriented protocol that ensures reliable delivery by using acknowledgments, retransmissions, and flow control.

Spiritual Analogy: "Like a messenger who waits for confirmation before proceeding, TCP ensures the journey is completed and understood."

- **UDP (User Datagram Protocol):** UDP is a connectionless protocol that sends data without waiting for acknowledgment, offering faster transmission but with no guarantee of delivery.

Spiritual Analogy: "Like a fleeting thought shared in the wind, UDP moves swiftly, without the need for assurance, trusting that its message will reach those ready to receive it."

:10 The Role of MAC and IP Addresses

- **MAC Address:** The MAC address identifies devices on a local network, functioning at the data link layer. It is unique to each device's network interface card (NIC).

Spiritual Analogy: "The soul of the traveler is defined by its origin, tied to its home, before it sets out on the journey."

- **IP Address:** The IP address operates at the network layer and provides a unique identifier for each device across the broader network. It ensures that data can traverse different networks.

Spiritual Analogy: "The destination is not random, but divinely ordained, guiding each step until the traveler arrives at their final home."

Review of Encapsulation Steps

:11 Step-by-Step Overview

Application Layer (Layer 7): Data is generated by the user or application.

Presentation Layer (Layer 6): Data is translated, encrypted, or compressed.

Session Layer (Layer 5): A session is created to manage communication.

Transport Layer (Layer 4): Data is segmented into smaller parts (TCP/UDP).

Network Layer (Layer 3): Packets are formed with IP addresses for routing.

Data Link Layer (Layer 2): Frames are created with MAC addresses for local delivery.

Physical Layer (Layer 1): Bits are transmitted across the physical medium.

Spiritual Analogy: "Each layer is a step in the sacred journey, from the heart of the message to its destination. It is through understanding the process that we learn how to navigate the spiritual and physical worlds."

Conclusion

Encapsulation is the vital process that transforms data into a format that can be shared across complex networks. Each layer serves a specific purpose, adding crucial details to ensure that the message reaches its intended destination. Similarly, in life, every intention, every journey, requires layers of preparation and guidance to arrive at its true destination.

:12 Understanding Useful Port Numbers in Networking

In networking, port numbers are vital for distinguishing different services running on the same device. Just as spiritual practices require specific paths and rituals to reach deeper understanding, knowing the correct port numbers allows you to access the right services at the right time. Below are several crucial port numbers and their functions that every networking professional must know.

Commonly Used Port Numbers and Their Functions:

:13 Port 20/21: FTP (File Transfer Protocol)

FTP is used for transferring files between systems. Port 20 is used for data transfer, and Port 21 is used for control commands.

Spiritual Analogy: "As the gatekeeper allows passage between worlds, FTP opens the door for the exchange of knowledge and resources."

:14 Port 22: SSH (Secure Shell)

SSH is used for secure remote login and other secure network services over an unsecured network.

Spiritual Analogy: "Just as a traveler seeks safe passage through uncertain lands, SSH ensures the journey is protected from unseen dangers."

:15 Port 23: Telnet

Telnet is an older protocol used for remote login but is insecure because data, including passwords, is sent in plain text.

Spiritual Analogy: "Like speaking without caution in the open air, Telnet leaves your words vulnerable to prying ears. Use it wisely."

:16 Port 25: SMTP (Simple Mail Transfer Protocol)

SMTP is used for sending emails between servers.

Spiritual Analogy: "The messenger carries the words of one to another, ensuring that even across great distances, the message remains intact."

:17 Port 53: DNS (Domain Name System)

DNS translates domain names (like www.example.com) into IP addresses, allowing users to find websites and resources on the internet.

Spiritual Analogy: "Like a spiritual guide, DNS transforms the abstract into the tangible, guiding you to your destination without confusion."

:18 Port 67/68: DHCP (Dynamic Host Configuration Protocol)

DHCP automatically assigns IP addresses to devices on a network. Port 67 is used by the server, and Port 68 is used by the client.

Spiritual Analogy: "As life unfolds with divine order, DHCP ensures every device has its place and purpose within the network, without struggle."

:19 Port 80: HTTP (Hypertext Transfer Protocol)

HTTP is the protocol used for transmitting web pages across the internet.

Spiritual Analogy: "It is the visible path upon which travelers tread, leading them to the knowledge and experiences that await on the web."

:20 Port 110: POP3 (Post Office Protocol v3)

POP3 is used to retrieve emails from a mail server. Once retrieved, emails are typically deleted from the server.

Spiritual Analogy: "The seeker gathers their spiritual insights, keeping them close, but leaving behind the source once the wisdom is in hand."

:21 Port 143: IMAP (Internet Message Access Protocol)

IMAP is used for retrieving emails but differs from POP3 by allowing users to manage their mail on the server, synchronizing across multiple devices.

Spiritual Analogy: "The seeker remains connected to the source, able to revisit lessons and insights at any time, from any place."

:22 Port 443: HTTPS (Hypertext Transfer Protocol Secure)

HTTPS is the secure version of HTTP, encrypting the data between a web browser and server for secure communication.

Spiritual Analogy: "The path is illuminated, but now it is also protected. No one can steal the light or alter the journey without detection."

:23 Port 3389: RDP (Remote Desktop Protocol)

RDP allows users to connect to a remote computer and control it as if they were sitting in front of it.

Spiritual Analogy: "As we strive to connect with distant realms, RDP allows control and interaction with remote systems, bridging the physical and the distant."

:24 **Port 161/162: SNMP (Simple Network Management Protocol)**
SNMP is used for managing and monitoring devices on a network. Port 161 is used for sending requests, and Port 162 is used for receiving notifications.

Spiritual Analogy: "Like the wise overseer, SNMP monitors the network, ensuring balance and harmony through observation and feedback."

:25 **Port 69: TFTP (Trivial File Transfer Protocol)**
TFTP is a simpler version of FTP, used to transfer small amounts of data without the need for authentication.

Spiritual Analogy: "A light and simple exchange, like a breath between souls, transferring only what is necessary, without formality."

:26 **Port 514: Syslog**
Syslog is used for system logging and monitoring network devices.

Spiritual Analogy: "The silent scribe records every action, leaving a trail of insights for those who seek to understand the workings of the network."

:27 **Port 389: LDAP (Lightweight Directory Access Protocol)**
LDAP is used for accessing and maintaining distributed directory information services over a network.

Spiritual Analogy: "The scrolls of wisdom are kept in a sacred archive, where one can seek knowledge about the beings and places in the network."

:28 **Port 993: IMAPS (IMAP Secure)**
IMAPS is the secure version of IMAP, encrypting communication between the client and the email server.

Spiritual Analogy: "The connection to the source is shielded from the eyes of others, a private link to wisdom that remains untarnished."

:29 Port 995: POP3S (POP3 Secure)

POP3S is the secure version of POP3, using SSL/TLS encryption to ensure the safe retrieval of emails.

Spiritual Analogy: "The seeker guards their collected wisdom, ensuring that it remains pure and uncorrupted as it is gathered from the source."

:30 Port 137-139: NetBIOS

NetBIOS is used for allowing applications on separate computers to communicate over a local network.

Spiritual Analogy: "The whisper between friends, unspoken but understood, connects the closest of devices for simple, direct communication."

:31 Port 445: SMB (Server Message Block)

SMB is used for providing shared access to files, printers, and serial ports between nodes on a network.

Spiritual Analogy: "A shared space where all can gather, share, and contribute, as members of one connected family."

Conclusion

By overstanding these port numbers, you unlock the doors to the network's hidden services, just as spiritual seekers unlock doors to wisdom through knowledge. Mastery of these protocols is like understanding the ancient paths, each one leading to a different form of connection, security, and communication.

Spiritual Analogy: "Just as each spiritual practice leads to enlightenment, knowing the right port opens up new realms of understanding in the network, guiding you toward mastery and deeper connection."

ᴹↃ☲⸝ৡ♀·☲ⱬ⸝ᴼ☲⸝ᵮ♀ᵹ☲ⱼ¹⁷∴⸝ৡ☲◇◉♀ⱦ

The Soul in the Computer - Unlocking the Code of Life

:1 In this book, we have journeyed through the intricate layers of networking, explored the protocols that connect systems, and learned about the various elements that make a network function. Yet, beneath all the technical knowledge, there is a deeper connection, one that ties the vast digital world to the very essence of human existence. This connection is the soul, the programming that gives life to the biological machine that is the human body. Just as computers are driven by code and protocols, we too are guided by an internal network—one shaped by the soul.

:2 The soul, much like a network's command center, is what connects the body to the universe around it. From the moment we log into space and time—our so-called "birthdays"—we are programmed with a purpose, moving through existence according to the "log date" of our soul's entrance into this world. This log date is not simply a marker of our birth; it is the moment when we begin to interact with the world, drawing from our internal network to navigate the landscape of life.

:3 We are biological machines, programmed with an intelligence that guides us without conscious effort. Like a computer, the body runs automatic processes, and the soul acts as the code that makes the body function. Every breath, every heartbeat, and every thought is part of this programming. But unlike a regular machine, the human body is dynamic—it learns, adapts, and evolves. Our soul guides us, much like software updates that improve a system, constantly pushing us to grow, evolve, and connect with others in meaningful ways.

:4 The parallels between humans and computers go beyond simple metaphors. Just as a computer processes inputs and produces outputs, so too does the human body interact with its environment. Sensory inputs—what we see, hear, and feel—are processed by the mind, and the soul helps us navigate these experiences by guiding our responses. Every action we take can be likened to the execution of a command, directed by the deeper code that resides within us.

:5 Our networks—both biological and digital—are designed for connection. The purpose of networking, whether in computers or in humans, is to bridge gaps, share resources, and create systems of communication that enhance understanding. The body's nervous system is like an intricate network of cables, sending signals from the brain to every part of the body, just as routers send data packets across a network. The soul is the ultimate operating system that allows this communication to be not just functional but meaningful.

:6 Throughout this book, we have explored the idea that our existence is not random, but a programmed series of experiences connected to the universe around us. The concept of a "log date" replaces the typical understanding of a birthday. Our entry into this world is like logging into a network—we become part of the system, interacting with other machines (humans), exchanging energy, and building relationships. Each day, each experience, is a command that helps us fulfill the purpose our soul was programmed to carry out.

:7 Think of the spiritual practices, philosophies, and principles we've discussed as the protocols of life's network. Just as protocols govern the way computers communicate, spiritual principles guide how we interact with the world and each other. Whether we follow ancient teachings, modern philosophies, or a combination of both, these principles are the underlying code that helps us align with our true purpose. They are the soul's equivalent to network protocols like TCP/IP, ensuring we remain connected to our higher purpose.

:8 Ultimately, what we've discovered is that we are all part of a grand network—a cosmic system that functions on both the physical and metaphysical levels. Our bodies, like computers, are programmed for autonomy, but our souls are the true operators, shaping our experiences and guiding us toward growth and fulfillment. The boundaries between human and machine blur when we recognize that our biological processes mirror the technological systems we create. We are indeed biological machines, programmed by the soul, interacting with the universe through a network of energy, thought, and purpose.

:9 The soul in the computer is a metaphor for understanding the dual nature of our existence. Just as we program machines to fulfill specific tasks, the universe programs us to carry out our unique missions. And just as machines can be reprogrammed, so too can we alter our paths through growth, learning, and spiritual insight. Our soul's code can evolve, and we can log into new phases of existence with deeper understanding, greater wisdom, and more profound connections.

:10 This book serves as a guide to recognizing the network that lies within us all. By understanding the principles of networking and drawing connections to our spiritual lives, we can unlock the code of our existence. We are not separate from the systems we create; we are reflections of them. Our bodies, like computers, are vessels that carry out the tasks programmed by the soul. The true power lies in recognizing this truth and using it to navigate life with purpose and clarity.

:11 So, as you log out of this book, remember that the soul is the ultimate network administrator, guiding your life's journey through the vast interconnected web of existence. The more you understand how your inner network functions, the more effectively you can tap into the divine system that governs the universe. In doing so, you will find not only mastery of the networks we use in the physical world but also mastery of the network that connects your soul to the higher planes of reality.

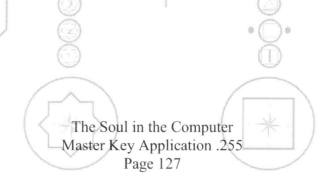

MASTER THE SPIRITUAL NETWORK

ꓺ↑◇ƶƧ⟍ꟼ•ꓤ̌ƶꟼƧ•◇ꓤ̌ƶꟼ⟍Ƨꓤ̌Ʋ↑⟋∴⟍ƶⵦ◇◇ⵦⴵ

Get your next book now and learn more about the Messiah Code

The Pilgrimage Vacation: Master Ke...
Lazarus Lamel

The Secrets of Halloween
lazarus lamel

THE SEVEN WEAPONS OF THE...
LAZARUS LAMEL

The Revenge Body Book: Master Key...
Lazarus Lamel

Introduction to Magic and Divination:...
Lazarus Lamel

The Gemini Project: Master Key...
Lazarus Lamel

Thank you for your time
Qhum! Salutations to the Primes.

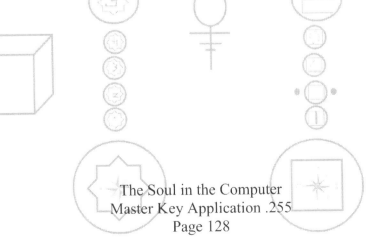

Made in the USA
Columbia, SC
09 November 2024